If your life were a movie,

what genre would you choose to binge on?

To my husband,
for the love we continue to build.
To all the couples
who nurture that spark
in their own relationships.
For those just starting with this book,
here's to a journey worth taking.

Get In or Get Out
But Don't Stay in the Freakn' Middle

By Dr. Lia A. Roth, Psya.D.© 2025

A F. Freud Series

A publication of LR^2 and the A.U.T.O.N.O.M.Y. Project

Editorial Campanadas

Buenos Aires - Argentina

ISBN: 978-1-951010-28-7

Photograph by Maria Ladrón de Guevara

Get in touch at https://drliaroth.com/getinorgetout

Index

PROLOGUE

I had a front-row seat to betrayal after my parents passed away, and let me tell you: it doesn't just sting, it shatters. It leaves you staring at a version of yourself you barely recognize.

When I picked up a book on betrayal that described it as simply a breaking of trust, I felt it didn't even begin to capture what I'd been through. Betrayal tears apart the foundation of who you thought you were and leaves you asking the hardest question of all: *"What now?"*

Writing became my way of healing. What I thought would be a single chapter on infidelity in a different book took on a life of its own. Growing bigger, louder, and more alive until it demanded its own stage. That's how this book came to be.

Yes, it started with betrayal. Yet in its process of growing, it became something more: a guide to becoming your own person next to someone else, and learning to love without losing yourself again.

I've spent years writing about shame. It was the topic of my dissertation and a major focus of my clinical work. My perspective? It's refreshingly different: emotions aren't here to bother us. They exist for a reason.

..and that reason isn't just homeostasis or balance.

It's survival.

We're constantly surviving at two levels: as biological and social beings. Once we grasp that, everything shifts. It opens up a whole new way of understanding ourselves and the world we live in, what I call *being* and *belonging*.

Guess what? When you start seeing infidelity through that same lens, something wild happens. Like with any type of severe betrayal, infidelity stops being just the wrecking ball of your life and turns into the launchpad. It's here to help you reset, rebuild, and rise higher than you ever thought you could.

As reviewers put it, this book isn't just about infidelity, it's about waking the hell up. It's for anyone who's been crushed, ghosted, or stuck in heart-pain. A blueprint for stepping into your boldest, most unapologetic self. And a reminder: you can love without bleeding yourself dry. You can rebuild without begging. Joy isn't lost, you just stopped looking in the right direction.

I want you to understand, the ego is your self-feeling, a story you tell yourself and others, and the reflection of how you believe others see you. Egos are dynamic, shaped by relationships and shared dreams. That's why infidelity hits so hard. When someone so close to you breaks that bond, it rips through the framework that holds you up. Betrayal doesn't just break trust. It wrecks your ego. It shakes the very fabric of who you believe you are.

I started this healing path when my sister Lilly, who had been betrayed at the same time I was, called me and said, "Mom and Pop had three daughters. But I only have one sister, and that is you!" Since then, we've been working together, helping people gain autonomy and start a new chapter in their lives.

Lilly doesn't just bring her wealth of experience in crisis management, there's more. The love of her life cheated on her with a doppelgänger. Mind-blowing, right?

Together, we uncovered something crucial: forgiveness isn't about patching up a shared story with someone who hurt you. It's about reclaiming your power, releasing the pain, and shifting your energy toward rebuilding a life that feels steady, whole, and undeniably yours.

Socrates, way back in 470/469 BCE, believed wisdom was central to happiness, and he was right. Yet here we are, still chipping away at our integrity, all to avoid conflict or discomfort. Still letting fear of rejection, perfectionism, and anxiety distract us from the wisdom we already carry within. For centuries, we've been chasing short-term gains, and somehow, we still haven't learned the lesson!

What makes this book different? It doesn't just redefine betrayal, it flips the narrative on its head. Forget the idea of patching things and reconciliation, which rarely lasts. Infidelity and any type of severe betrayal demand nothing less than a full reset that starts from within.

You can read this book in a couple of hours...

...or you can dive in and work through it until its message becomes part of you.

That's when this book goes beyond words and tools.

It lifts you, and makes sure you never end up in the same mess again.

Together, we'll dig into bold frameworks like the binary relationship theory and the concept of self-betrayal, revealing how these patterns pave the way for bigger betrayals.

When you stay loyal to yourself and cut out self-betrayal, the risk of getting blindsided shrinks fast. Autonomy becomes your secret weapon, a wisdom that transforms how you approach love, connection, and your own identity.

...And optimism? It's not optional. This isn't the end of your story. As Nietzsche said, *What does not kill you makes you stronger.* This bump in the road might just be the universe nudging you toward your full potential.

So, buckle up. Let's reset, rebuild, and rise into the next chapter of your life.

Dr. Lia A. Roth, St. Louis, MO - December 2024

My mother once told me,
"If you want to make music,
you have to face the piano."
That's when it hit me,
I was going to make myself happy.

1- Proud & Binary

Are you sensitive for the title of this chapter? Yes, binary thinking has gotten a bad rap lately. And honestly, it's not even binary's fault! It's more about people misunderstanding what binary really is.

We think it's about two elements, right? Wrong. It's never been about two: it's about three. You see, when you only have two elements, they end up reflecting each other. They are stuck together. They create a mirror, and mirroring often brings rivalry. Think of this: give vs. take, big vs. small, pleasure vs. displeasure, active vs. passive.

There's no real interplay, just tension. But throw in a third element?

Now we're talking!

That's where the magic happens. Where things can actually move, shift, and grow.

When you add a third element, everything changes. Those two pieces -0 and 1- they are no longer mere opposites, locked in some mirror-rivalry. It's the relationship between them that makes everything work. That connection turns duality into something much bigger, something that can evolve and grow. It's no longer one or the other; it's a whole system. Truthful, guess what? That's what sex is.

Sex is not a state you reach. It's a practice, something dynamic and alive. It's not about crossing some finish line where you have "arrived, here is your letter!" More about living in the in-between, where things move and shift.

The truth is, anyone who embraces a letter -whether it's M, F, or anything else, has to learn how to be in this world as themselves. That whole idea of "coming out"? Well that is not limited to a certain few. We all go through it at some point in life. It's that moment when you tell your parents, friends, and whoever the heck wants to listen: "Hey, I'm my own person." It's terrifying, but it's also freakn' liberating.

No matter how difficult that moment is, know this: coming out is only the start. It's not the grand finale, only the opening act. Putting a label on yourself is one thing; living it is another. Living it takes work. Serious work. Confusion, hesitation, disappointment... they are all part of the process. Joy and pleasure are too.

I remember a friend of mine who flew to Florida for surgery. While she was away, I took care of her dog. When she came back to pick him up, I opened the door to let her into my apartment. That place, ohhh! ...I can still picture it. Huge windows facing west, where the sunsets transformed the evenings into life's celebrations, gentle reminders to slow down and simply *be*.

We sat down while the coffee brewed in the kitchen, filling the air with its rich, familiar aroma. A moment later, that final gurgle of the pot signaled it was ready. Leaving her on the couch, playing with her dog, I went to fetch two cups. That dog couldn't contain himself, bouncing back and forth, tail wagging so hard it practically sliced through the silence.

As I returned to the living room, I caught her looking at me. Her gaze wasn't casual; it lingered, heavy with something unsaid.

I handed her the sugar bowl and a spoon. She took it. The porcelain clink filling the room. I felt the moment tighten. She stood there, one breath away from spilling what had changed with her.

I didn't need to hear it. I raised my eyes, meeting hers: "I know," I said, the words landing like a whisper in the stillness.

I watched her go from nervous -like anyone about to spill the beans would be- to almost buzzing with excitement for her orchiectomy. While her hands fidget, her eyes showed this particular glow, as if that future she had started to live a few days ago couldn't come fast enough.

After a few weeks? Reality hit.

That electric anticipation she'd been building for years gave way to something quieter, heavier. The finish line she thought she had crossed was only a starting point.

Life is not about arriving, it's all about the journey. She still had to figure out what it truly meant to live as her real self. That's the hard part we all have to face one way or another. The part no one really talks about, and what lingers long after wounds or bandages come off.

So, here's the deal: Be whoever the heck you wanna be. But be proud, because it's never easy. Understand that you are practicing being you. You are learning how it feels.

Didn't get it right the first time? So, what? No big deal. You are practicing, after all. Try again. Failure is not in the choices you've made. The real failure is living a life that never felt like yours to begin with.

2- You, Me & the Relationship

One day I told my sister, Lilly, that I thought healthy relationships are never made of two, but three: you, me and the relationship between us. You have probably heard her say this on one of our lives.

I suppose now I get to explain what I meant by that, right? The point is this, in today's world, there are very few brave souls who don't have something personal other than being something to their special someone. Most stay-at-home moms, dads, partners often have side gigs, trades or hobbies that are theirs. We all tackle this business of living in our own way, creating an identity that goes beyond just being someone's partner.

More than that, we harbor our own dreams, too, about what we want to achieve, goals to reach, and the legacy we want to leave behind for our children... Even if those dreams feel a bit scary at times.

In a binary model, once you are your own person, you truly get to be your own person. It's not a destination. Not an arrival point, more of a journey that is built through the gestures of everyday life. Never a grand display. More like an accumulation of tiny, consistent, steps that show curiosity, courage and commitment.

If you want to be an artist, don't get caught up in the idea that you need a bunch of expensive equipment. You don't need the perfect setup, as much as you need the passion to come forward as an artist in training. I bet you already have a couple of things at home that you could use to get started.

Like Daniel, who wanted to be an architect. He was going to college, but every exam required him to make 3D models of houses, and he didn't have the money for all the expensive materials. Did that stop him? Not even close. He found what he needed in the trash outside a fancy paper shop, and no one ever noticed. His models were top-notch. Passion has that particular way of opening doors for you.

We all have different yearnings and zest for life. Many of us also crave a life companion. Someone who is there, standing by our side through better or worse, richer or poorer, in sickness and in health, as we grow old together... So, why not have it all??

That's the real thrill of a binary relationship: you, me, and the electric dance between us. Scratch the idea of togetherness as being scrambled into one. Nope! That's the old patriarchal nuclear family mindset.

...And lately? It has been working against us.

Time for an upgrade!

Instead, embrace a togetherness rooted in shaping your identities with fierce determination and steadfastness. Supported, admired, deeply connected, yet never losing yourself in the process. A dance that honors both your unity and your undeniable individuality.

3- Working Hard Towards Somebody Else's Dream

It starts like a dream, right? You are hustling to work because, hey, med school isn't cheap. Despite your parents are pitching in, you still need extra cash.

You are hurrying to work, mentally ticking through your to-do list, a stack of papers clutched in one hand, coffee in the other. The city's alive around you, horns blaring, people weaving past, all moving to some invisible rhythm. But you? You are on your own track, barely noticing anything outside your own bubble.

And then, bam! A gust of wind comes out of nowhere, yanking the papers right out of your grip. Pages scatter, darting across the street like they've got a mind of their own. You scramble, grabbing at sheets, feeling the panic set in. Yet as you reach for another stray page, a hand joins yours. Someone's there, helping you catch the runaway papers.

You look up, and there it is smiling at you. No words, just this warm, quiet smile that cuts through the morning rush. For a second, the world goes quiet, like it's just you two in the middle of that busy street. Your bubble? Officially popped.

You both straighten up, papers back in hand, and share a brief nod before going your separate ways. You rush to the office, brushing it off like nothing. Yet the energy from that moment sticks with you, a spark that follows you through the day.

Then, was it that same night or a few days later? You are out with friends, and, like the universe is playing matchmaker, you bump into the same person again. Jay Whozit. In one fluke moment, your whole world shifts.

That passionate lightning hits you hard, like your life has been sprinkled with magic. You look at this person, and just like that, they become your everything. Your hero, Jay Whozit. Your reason for waking up in the morning.

It feels so perfect, so right, that imagining a future together is easy ...and before you know it, you are married, working tirelessly to make it work, to become "one."

Then, real life kicks in (...and let's be honest, life is messy, frustrating, and nothing like those moonlit walks or whispered sweet nothings you see in movies).

No, reality shows up with its bills, tuition fees, and no room for two dreams. So, you compromise. You take a back seat, offering to wait for your turn, putting your loved one's dream first.

Slowly, passion fades into routine. You are biting your tongue more often than not, just to keep the peace. You start noticing things you didn't see before. Those cute little quirks you once adored, now they irritate you. They show you how different the two of you are. Your partner is staying out late, claiming it's for a project or some work thing.

... and remember that red sweater you bought? Still in the bag, untouched. Not the first time, either. You have given gifts, made efforts, and yet, here you are: left behind, feeling like a forgotten memory.

You work hard to make this person happy. You have taken on extra shifts to provide the things your partner loves. Yet, all that effort does not grant you a smile. You never get it right. No matter how much you give, it never seems to be enough. You are worn thin, drained from trying so hard to be the thing that finally fills them up, to make your better half smile with joy by your side. As if your love could fix what they never learned to hold for themselves.

How is that somehow, despite everything, you still feel that pull? That smile still melts you down, and there's a part of you that is proud to be Jay Whozit's partner. You tell yourself that togetherness is about commitment, and you take on the challenge.

Here's one big truth about commitment: it is never glamorous. It's hard, bittersweet work. More than anything, it is a compromise that can leave you swallowing your pride over and over again. You have gone from waking up feeling lucky to have them by your side as you stare across the room, wondering if you should stick around for another day. It does not feel like a team any longer. More like two people coexisting. Roommates, fading into strangers under the same roof.

Years have passed, and guess what? You are still not back in college. You have realized you are not living your dream. The smiles, the joys? They've become shallow, almost rehearsed. Then it hits you: you have been working tirelessly towards making your loved one's dream possible,... and you are not even good at it.

Many times, when two people merge into one, it means one person sacrifices their life. More than that, this oblation is taken for granted. Ever been there? You start with love so deep you think, "I'll give everything for this person." Before you know it, you actually are giving exactly your everything.

One of you is living the dream while the other one is hanging on, waiting for their turn, in charge of real life and working hard to keep the relationship going, but frustrated and not even aware why.

Here's the truth: love shouldn't be tested like that. When one person feels like they are giving up too much, resentment will eventually sneak in, and that's a tough feeling to shake off.

It was never your responsibility to make someone else's dream come true. Sure, we all want to support the people we love, nevertheless you can't carry their life on your back. That's too much weight for anyone. It's tempting, though, right? You think, "If I only give a little more... try a little harder... sacrifice a bit more..." as if you were doing something wrong. It is not your failure.

Those thoughts tend to pop up when things are already starting to crumble, don't they? When you are not just taking on your partner's dreams, but the weight of the entire household's happiness. So, you work even harder. No longer with joyful interest, in any case out of lack of alternatives and hoping it'll fix things.

Yes, once again you are thinking this is somehow landing on your shoulders.

Let me ask you, how's the appreciation for your hard work been so far?

So, why more of the same would work any better?

Your partner's dream is theirs to chase, as much as yours is yours. Love isn't about one person bending over backward to make everything work. It's about both people walking their own path, while nurturing the relationship as a third entity, something that belongs to both of you. Because you will never build your legacy if you keep sacrificing yourself for someone else. Rather, you will end up feeling empty, and that's not love. That's losing yourself.

4- Lip Service & Let Downs

When passion fades into routine, and you find yourself pouring energy into someone else's dream, it feels like a gut punch. You wonder, "*How did I get here?*" But the real question is: what are you going to do next?

Staying stuck in the middle is draining, directionless. Time to pick a path and put yourself first. Constantly bargaining with your dreams, quietly shelving what matters to you or settling for less, that is not love. That is survival mode. You are done with living at half-capacity, done with being the last straw, stretched thin and taken for granted. Now, you are stepping into a life that's fully yours.

It's time for some serious self-reflection, the kind that only happens after you have run through the usual string of questions: *How did this all happen? When did I start losing myself? Why are they taking advantage of me? Why do I do this to myself? When did I let my dreams take a back seat? How many dreams have I given up on... and at what cost?*

Then it dawns on you, you have been endlessly giving in a world full of takers. It wasn't just your career you sacrificed. You constantly put your partner, your friends, and even people you barely know ahead of yourself.

When someone's always in front of you, that means you are usually behind them. If no one's behind you, it means you are the last straw, stretched thin and about to break. Working tirelessly towards somebody else's dream.

Take a few deep breaths to calm yourself down. It's bad, but it feels scarier than it is.

It's not going to be easy, however, once you get a handle on that mental hamster wheel spinning out of control, you will come to this conclusion. You need to think forward.

Now that you see it, the next step is reclaiming your direction. No more autopilot, no more wondering how you ended up here. This is where you start channeling your energy into something that matters to you. This time, the path is yours.

Go, get your notepad and pencil, make a nice cup of tea and think hard. Consider what do you need to build a life that fills you up. Take a hard look at what drives you, what excites you, and what it would mean to pursue that every day of your life.

Then, go deeper: What do you need to start doing to make it happen? Maybe it's carving out time for your goals and saying 'yes' to opportunities you've been too afraid to take on.

Next, admit it, you cannot expect anything to change if you keep doing the same stuff. Ask yourself the second crucial question: What do you need to stop doing? What are the things that distract you from your path, and that you need to let go of to reach your potential, your goals, your woo? Write it all down, because clarity is the first step to transformation. This is your commitment to yourself.

Ready? The following step is having 'the conversation.'

It won't be easy, but it's absolutely doable. It's got to happen.

You need to lay down your cards. Share what's really going on, what you need, and the changes that have to be made.

Take a moment to be totally honest. If the balance is skewed and you are the one always giving, that's simply not sustainable. It's also what brought you to this turning point.

The real strength in relationships starts with the one you build with yourself. It's about starting to define your sense of self. You do not need to know all the answers or to have clear perfect goals. What you need is that inner compass, which is the spirit to explore and take bold steps. It's about negotiating terms that feel right for you, so you can begin to navigate life on your own terms.

If this feels uncomfortable, good... Growth is supposed to stretch you.

Besides, I know how strong and capable you are.

How do I know? Because you've been running the show from day one, right?

Well!! Time to get real.

Here is what balance looks like. Right after I moved to the USA, a married friend of mine told me, 'Great, I'm coming to visit!' Without thinking twice about all the things that kept her being her in Buenos Aires, she just decided not to miss the opportunity. Now, out of mutual respect and care for her husband, she still nurtured that third element. She invited him to come along. That's the binary model in action: showing up fully as yourself while also honoring the relationship as a shared, dynamic creation.

When you have some clarity on who you are, you can show up fully, ready to meet another whole person and create something even better for you both.

It takes a while to find the determination, the right words, the right moment. Once you pour your heart out and lay your cards on the table, everything starts to shift.

Here I would say, relationships have two big camps: those who truly listen, and those who don't. Some partners are the real deal. They mean every word. You will notice it in the actions they take after the conversation. They have tuned into your needs, your pain. They love you and want the best for you. Your happiness makes them happy.

Then there are the smooth talkers. They say all the right things: "I support you," "We'll make this work." They will flash that smile, give you a hug, and for a moment, you feel closer than you have been in a long, long time.

But then... nothing.

Days stretch into weeks, and it's all still the same.

Not a single sign of hope.

It is still you running in circles, while your needs are still collecting dust on the shelf. The worst part? When they don't make a move, you might find yourself slipping right back into your usual roles like nothing ever happened.

At the turf, only the horse that crosses the finish line first gets the big prize. It doesn't matter how close the others come, there's no trophy for almost making it. Same goes for relationships: words and promises might sound sweet, but with no real follow-through, no one's really winning.

...When nobody is winning chances are you are the one taking the loss.

Worse yet, this is the trap of the traditional, nuclear family setup, where "togetherness" is just code for you giving up more of yourself.

Enter the binary theory of relationships, where each person still keeps their own fire lit. It's a world apart from you being the only one keeping the togetherness candle burning while everyone else lounges on the sidelines.

This is where things get rough. When words don't back up actions, trust goes hollow ...and a hollow trust? That's just a breeding ground for new resentments. You end up feeling invisible, like you are shouting into the void while your dreams go stale, and you are left wondering, was this ever about 'us' at all?

Until one day, you catch yourself fantasizing about a life in a parallel universe. A universe where you actually achieved all those things you once dreamed of, like finishing medical school. You don't act on it, but guilt creeps in as you sit there, watching movies, scrolling through photos, and reminiscing about the good times with people you haven't seen in years. Maybe you even look them up online, a bittersweet pinprick that stings more than you'd like to admit.

Lost in your world of 'what ifs' and 'could-have-beens,' something suddenly yanks you back to reality.

A late-night ping on your partner's phone.

Harmless, right?

Except... it is not. You glance over, not thinking much of it, but then you see a name. You glance over a bit more. No one you recognize. Not a friend. Not a colleague. Your stomach tightens, and curiosity takes hold. Before you know it, the phone is in your hand.

That's when the floor falls out from under you and the air leaves the room. A cascade of messages. Flirty, daring, playful, each one more suggestive than the last, hitting you like a slap. Then, the final blow: a picture. The kind that doesn't need a caption, that tells a story you never wanted to read. Your chest tightens a bit more, pulse racing, your breath stutters. Everything you knew, or thought you knew, lays in limbo in an instant.

You can feel your heart pounding hard in your ears as your fantasy of a parallel universe collides with the cold, hard truth of this universe. This isn't a dream anymore. It's a nightmare you didn't see coming.

Or... did you?

Red pill or Blue pill?

Here's the deal:

Take the red pill, and you stay right where you are.

Comfortably uncomfortable. Stuck in the life you know, playing the same roles, spinning the same wheels, and wondering why nothing changes.

...Or take the blue pill, read the next chapters, and start unlocking the full potential of your life (and the responsibility that comes with it).

Growth isn't easy, but it's worth it.

So, what's it going to be?

5- Cracking the Code of Betrayal & Why It Shatters You

Spoiler alert: Is this a heavy chapter to read? Absolutely. But here's what no one ever told you, betrayal isn't just a break of trust. If that's all it was, tell me, why hasn't it been easy to just flip them the finger and move on? Exactly.

Because this runs way deeper.

Keep reading. What you are about to learn? It's going to change everything.

This book dives into infidelity, deceit, and the deepest kind of betrayal: self-betrayal. There are many forms of betrayal that life throws at us from every angle. It's unavoidable. What does that mean for us? It screams our need to master autonomy, and learning to stand strong in our own two feet.

Nope, retreating to a distant cave like a monk isn't the answer. That kind of isolation only sharpens the knife of self-betrayal, slicing away the life and potential you are meant to experience.

Before we unpack the heavy load of betrayal's blueprint, I need a quick favor. This one small step will make everything click later. Take a moment -right now- and draw a tree or a dog. If you don't have a pencil handy, engage with your imagination and trace it in the air with your finger.

Don't rush through it. More importantly, don't think, *I'll keep reading and come back to it later.* This exercise might feel simple, even playful, but it's the key to understanding what comes next.

So go ahead–pause, play with it, and actually do it. You'll see why soon enough.

How old is the tree or dog you draw?

Where is it located?

...so, in reality, between you and me, tell me: you kind of made this drawing based on a tree or a dog you've seen before and even known, right?

Good! Keep that in mind.

Next move? Let me spell out what severe betrayal is because, clearly, no one else has cracked the code. You are getting it fresh, straight from the oven of scientific insight, served up hot and ready to dive into. I know, bringing semiotics into the thick of this book can make your head spin. This time, your eyes will pop up open as you realize how all this works.

So, buckle up and grab a drink... a fancy one, not a cup of tea but a fancy one. We are about to dive into betrayal like never before.

Yes, this might leave you like, 'Wait, what? I need to read that again.'

No worries, I'll be practically whisper-screaming it straight into your ear. Let me tell you, it will sink in... Eventually. When it does, you'll be left breathless, like a sudden rush of clarity crashing over your spine.

Everybody defines betrayal as a break of trust, right?

Let's dig deeper, what is trust, really? The short answer: trust is the experience of consistency that allows for anticipation. It's that smooth, steady flow, where everything just fits. Where everything keeps adding up without that sudden, awkward "Uh, what was that all about?" or "Where did that come from?" and "What do I do with this now?" moment. Trust is when it all clicks together seamlessly, which makes it a category of safety.

...because even when you "trust" things will go wrong, that's when you brace for impact. And that? That's safety too!

We Are Born Craving Bliss and Rejecting What Disrupts It

This is how it goes... Did you know that our very first emotion at birth is hate[1]? Think about it.

We come into this world crying, which makes emotion the very first thing we do in life. By the way, if we don't cry on our own, we get our first spank. Yeah, that spank is necessary to clear our lungs of amniotic fluid, but still, the point is... reality in its raw form stings.

---

[1] Carmen Gonzalez Táboas, personal communication.

Then, what happens? Suddenly, we find heaven. We are brought into our mother's[2] arms, and it's pure bliss. It is comforting, our first taste of belonging. It is warm, sweet, cozy, bigger than anything, and pushes us from hate to heaven in seconds.

That moment becomes our everything. We spend our lives chasing that feeling again, the need to belong to feel safe and sound. We dread being at the edge between here and there, from comfort zone to the unknown to conquer.

We don't fear rejection just because being an outcast isn't cool or because solitude feels boring. We fear it because most of us rely on others to help define who we are, and survive. Being alone can feel dangerous, like walking a tightrope without a safety net.

We are always juggling two realities at once, the biological and the social (or representational-social). One is raw instinct, flesh and bones, the stuff hardwired into our DNA. The other? It is all about connection, and the ever-evolving game of navigating the social world. The idea of who we are, and who we want to become... and how we come across to others. Because, as Charles Horton Cooley put it, there is a rich emotional value deeply tied to that mirroring we get through others.

---

[2] In psychology, mother is a role and a function, more than a person.

The space between where we are now and where we could be (if we snap out of autopilot) can feel daunting. Yet, it's pure potential, holding the seed of everything we can create.

Do you know what happens the moment we are born? We get tagged like priority mail: name, address, ID number. Stamped, processed, and ready to ship. No instructions included, just a one-way ticket into the chaos of life.

We don't have a sense of identity at birth. No consciousness, no ego. That all comes much later. Before, there needs to be an awakening of synaptic paths and developmental achievements. Nature knows what she's doing when we come into this world as unfinished business.

Before we start slapping labels on things with words and logic, we are explorers.

First lab? A babies mouth. We sniff, we touch, we taste, we feel, we cry. Each sensory perception sparking neural pathways.

We are baby scientists, building a universe from scratch, trying to figure out what everything is and where we fit in it. And here's where the pleasure principle kicks in: if it feels good, we claim it. If it doesn't? We spit it out, no second-guessing. Pleasure pulls us in, pain pushes us away[3]:

Feels good? Me.

Not nice? Hard pass.

It's that primal, that simple.

We are mapping out the world and ourselves, one tiny little experience at a time. Yes, it takes a while but eventually, we build up an ego. The perfect vantage point, our center of command. The spot where we finally gain a unique perspective on everything we've built from the ground up. The moment we stop just absorbing the world and start declaring:

"I want[4]"

... and point it out with a finger[5].

As infants, we believe grown-ups know best.

---

[3] Unless driven by masochism.

[4] That tiny phrase holds the birth of subjectivity. *I* stands for the self, a flicker of being. And *want*? That means there's a gap. A craving. A sense that something is missing. It's the first spark of the ego beginning to take shape. Before words, before rules, there's just the body saying: *I feel a lack, and I want it filled.*

[5] The baby points. Reaches. Grabs. Cries. The finger extends before the sentence forms. Because the body has its own way of speaking: it *wants*, it *asks*, it *demands*. That little gesture? It's not small. It's the ego waking up and the desire to fill the gap, to be seen, to be met.

Our survival 101? Read the room, follow the rules (or break them, but stay within adult's orbit). We become little experts at picking up grown-ups moods, expectations, and every unspoken "should." As Shakespeare, we take those wishes as our commands.

But growing up? That's a whole different game. Trust starts with self-trust. Love starts with self-love. Not everyone makes it this far. Plenty of people age without ever stepping into their own authority. The real achievement? Learning to trust your own reality, instead of reacting to someone else's.

What you call gut feeling? That is your intuition in action. Built on this sensory groundwork you have been laying since day one. Picking up on gestures, emotions, and all those tiny, invisible signals most people miss. Your intuition knows the vibes. It's your early warning system in action. Something that forms long before logic ever steps in.

What Holds You Together

Do you know why we come into this world immature? Because the ability to label things with words is absolutely key to developing our sense of self, and all what it means to be a person. Language and culture help us build our mental framework.

Yeah, yeah, I know, most people think we use language just to talk. You know, English, German, Spanish... sure, those are part of it. But language is so much more than that.

Let me explain here, at risk of being lengthy and too psychoanalytic, that language is more than a system of rules for processing, expressing, and understanding meaning. It extends beyond communication and speaking. It's the invisible architecture that holds together our thoughts, emotions, and identities so that they take shape. Language is the framework through which we create, navigate and make sense of the world.

Language becomes the medium through which we construct reality, shaping how we see ourselves, the world, and how we relate to others. Language is there as we create our subjectivity, and its effect on us pushes us to pursue what always feels just out of reach.

Language starts with what I call the maternal language, and describe as fused and fusing, in a state of becoming. Fused and fusing, means there's no "me" or "you.". No contradictions, no limits, just endless possibility, like a wave still part of the ocean of amniotic fluid.

First comes the baby's babble, rich with preverbal, sensory experience. In those early sounds, the infant exists in a state of undivided wholeness with the mother. A fused dyad, held within the Imaginary register.[6]

Then, the thinking mind steps in, and the rupture of entering the Symbolic order takes place.

Have you ever heard of the mirror stage? The infant once played with the mirror. Now, they recognize that reflection as self. The child 'realizes' it's an individual and starts using language in a different way.

Did you notice that to make sense, you have to say one word at a time? No more fused and fusing, no more babbling language, just like a person is its own individual, every word, every idea now stands on its own while still being part of a bigger picture.

One word at a time, all lined up by grammar's rules, so your ideas actually connect with others.

What happens when ideas are not lined up? Ah.. that is fertile ground for hesitation, contradiction, ambivalence, confusion... You name it.

People are like words, on their own, they don't mean much. Think about it. If I say "red," you'd wait for more

---

[6] See Bion's (1967) work to understand the distinction between beta elements (as a pre-symbolic melding of sensations) and their transformation into alpha elements through maternal reverie, where the mother serves as a head that thinks the baby's projections. Once within the symbolic order, the individual increasingly takes on this function, working through sensations and meaning to situate themselves in relation to their inner world and their place in context.

...red what? If I say "cold," your mind instantly considers "hot" to get it. We make sense through connection, just like words do.

We are only a part of a bigger picture that defines us.

Yes, we go through different stages as we mature. But that doesn't mean everything we've left behind is no longer in use. We just prioritize what is in use.

Beyond our awareness, we constantly function at two levels. What I call the fused and fusing maternal language acts as emotional intelligence, shaping meaning. Whereas we use the symbolic logic of rational thinking to gain understanding.

This also means that, at a certain level of awareness[7], our past and future coexist, and the distinction between inside and outside blurs, following the same internal logic.

In truth, our mind operates more like a quantum model than the simplified, straight line system of symbolic logic. We rely on this updated system to navigate, understand, strategize, and survive in more advanced environments, doing a solo job while being a part of society.

[7] Perceived past, present and future

So, What is Language Then?

As I said, language is the framework, the structural foundation that keeps everything about "you" standing upright. It holds the entire building of who you feel you are, put together brick by brick as a person.

The smallest building block of language is called the sign. A sign is a two-sided thing -like yin and yang- both parts working together in sync.

One side called the signifier (or "auditory image" if we're being fancy), is like a treasure chest. It's packed with all the sensory experiences you have been collecting since day one.

That groundwork I keep mentioning? It lives here.

Everything you have touched, smelled, heard, and felt gets stored away, shaping how you see the world. It's your freakin' past.

That's how you know how to draw a dog or a tree.

It is how you know you like your meals a certain way.

...and how you can spot J. Whozit from a block away.

All those unconscious sensory experiences quietly hold up everything you do, and how you communicate.

Want it clearer?

When I asked you to draw a tree or a dog, I just used plain, universal words. To be able to respond, you brought up your personal experiences. The smell of the bark, the warmth of fur, the way it felt to touch and play with that dog or climb that tree. That sensory connection is what shapes the drawing in your head. What helps you decode communication every single time.

So, what's on the other side of the sign?

That's the signified: the concept.

The rational, logical side of the sign we build through social interactions. It's the shared understanding of what a tree or a dog is. The universal agreement we all nod along to.

...before we make it personal.

Yes, of course, it also works the other way. The signified is what lets us share our internal world with others–so they can connect to what we say we feel.

We are constantly doing that work, making sense of things, giving meaning, and trying to understand each other. Maybe even empathize.

Yeah, you guessed it, it takes a bit longer to achieve this signified side of the sign. Babies babble before they form words, and even when they start talking, a two-year-old's speech is a whole different beast compared to when they start to use logic and rational thinking as teenagers.

What really matters is that these two sides, the yin and yang of language called sign, never fly solo. The signifier and signified are always in sync, each one lifting the other up, making sense of the world together.

When you are chatting with your friends, reading, driving, your synaptic connections aren't just firing in your brain, they are lighting up your whole system. Your body and emotions are part of the conversation too.

When you talk about something, your body adds its own twist. You are not just sharing concepts (signified); you are expressing them in a way that's uniquely yours. That personal spark -the signifiers- comes from neural pathways you have reinforced through the years, lit by electrical impulses and hormones adding their own tone to the mix[8].

You don't just talk, read or watch a movie...

You fully engage in it, embodying the experience.

Even if you are just solving a math equation, it's meaningful to you, and your body is right there with you, bringing a breath, a shiver, a skipped heartbeat, or

---

[8] See Bion's (1967) work on beta elements as raw, sensory-affective experience that must be processed through alpha function to become thinkable.

a flushed cheek. When you speak, your words aren't just sounds. They carry your rhythm, your energy–your hands moving, your eyebrows lifting, your whole presence making that equation come alive for someone else.

Well, then, that's why we are born immature. Born with a body but far from complete. It takes years to shape our sense of self. Call it identity, call it ego. We are a story, a living, breathing narrative. Your own masterpiece in the making. This is how language finds its way into our bones, how it's embodied, and how time itself becomes part of the mix, sculpting us into who we are.

Did I mention the sign has two parts? Well, I kind of skipped a third element. There is a bar between these two sides called the bar of repression. It's like a boundary between you and everything around you.

That bar is there to remind you that you can never experience the world exactly as it is, only as you make it. And when it comes to expressing yourself, you can never do it fully. No matter how hard you try, something will always be left unsaid[9].

---

[9] In French psychoanalysis, it's call the Real, unreachable yet ever present.

The bar of repression between the signifier and the signified comes to remind us that there is a defensive mechanism at play. Repression is not the only defense we use. Consider denial, idealization, intellectualization and the many other ones at play in the reasons you have been keeping the red flags tucked away under the rug.

Basically, every sign[10] boils down three parts: an idea, an emotion, and an action, all working together while we juggle the signifier and the signified as we build a world to stand on.

...and all of this, every bit of it, happens on a timeline that is not linear:

Past - Present - Future

I mentioned before that the signifier treasures all the sensory data of our past experiences. It doesn't stop there. Every time we think, speak, or act, the past and future linger, tantalizing and teasing.

As I said before, we draw from our past to feed the signifier. But as we stand in the present, that past comes to visit us as we project onto the future. Sometimes, it's the fire under us, driving us toward a goal, a dream, a vision that screams *go for it!* Other times? It's the dead

---

[10] Or to be precise, every representation has three elements: an emotional charge, and -more than just action- a know-how of how to go about things, rooted in what Piaget called generalization.

weight, dragging us down, whispering, *Who do you think you are?* When hope, optimism, and belief in what's possible feel just out of reach.

Meaning doesn't just stem from past experiences. It is shaped by where we stand now -our self-confidence, expectations for the future, beliefs and emotions, the treasure chest we have built, our ability to open doors to new opportunities, and so much more.

Whether it's as simple as quenching your thirst or as thrilling as hitting the jackpot, the past, present, and future are always tangled up, entwined like passionate lovers, shaping the way we experience life, understand it, and make it profoundly meaningful.

All those little cues you cherished from being with Jay? The ones that built your idea of who Jay Whozit is and how it feels to be with Jay (the signifier), get stored up as neural connections. Trust grows as a visceral know-how by adding up all those cues that shape your idea of Jay... while tossing aside the bits that don't fit, that you are unsure about, or that just don't seem worth your time for the moment.

I mentioned before that the ego[11] is that vantage point, where you get to look at everything you have built from the ground up. It's where you start to see yourself not just as an individual, but as part of a shared story, one where Jay plays a key role in how you understand who you are. It also happens that Jay is a mirror to you.

Other than who is Jay and what Jay did, the most important thing is everything you have built around what being with Jay means to you. That personal side of the sign called signifier. That bond shapes your sense of self, your identity, and the life shared together.

The connection with Jay affects the core of who you are and how the world appears through your eyes. Jay is a key layer of your sense of self because you created a narrative of your life alongside Jay.

System Failure

Remember when I said language is the framework of the building that is your life? Well, betrayal is like a tempest that rips through your carefully constructed walls.

---

[11] For this book, I use *sense of self, ego,* and *I* interchangeably, referring to your core identity, how you see yourself and the mirroring self-value that you gather from your interactions and standing in the world. Just know these terms have precise and distinct meanings in different psychoanalytic theories.

Betrayal is when everything you believed about someone who mattered deeply, shatters. Suddenly, all that solid structure falls apart. Your past experiences can't help you make sense of what's unfolding, and you are unable to project yourself into the future. You are left stranded at the rock bottom of your present time. You can't think, can't act. All that's left is raw emotion pulsing through you.

In other words, betrayal strikes when the signifiers you have cherished lose their enchantment, the exact instant you realize it's all a lie. The memories you once held close, the solid foundation that shaped your sense of self, can crumble in an instant when their truth is revealed. When they show themselves as nothing more than a disguise, a lie.

The moment those special memories, the signifiers, become flat and powerless, you lose your grip. The personal logic[12] you organized to find pleasure despite life being messy. All that once kept you moving forward alongside your partner. All that crumbles.

---

[12] Are "shifts" in the jouissance possible? I believe that severe betrayal is a disruption. It can change the way we reach for the Other, how we pursue desire, engage with struggle, and move through life's highs and lows. You've probably seen it in people who survive life-altering events—whether illness, accident, or betrayal—where something at the core of their desire and way of being shifts. It's not just a surface change but a rewiring, reconfiguration of the logic that drives their choices, relationships, and experience of pleasure and pain.

It doesn't just cracks your ego, it leaves you speechless. Stuck in a present that is unimaginable.

Another Round

Here's the thing about language:

The signifiers (those sensory experiences, those "auditory images") anchor you into your inner world.

Meanwhile, signifieds (the concepts, the idea that the signifiers point to) link you to your outer world.

Let me say it again:

The signifiers are the embodiment of all that anchors you into your inner world. They are the treasure of experiences infused with memories, emotions, fantasies, desires, expectations, and the unspoken truths that shape your perception of reality.

While on the other side, coming from our surrounding, our culture, our interactions with people... we have the signifieds that keep you connected to your outer world.

This part is tricky to show, so I'll give a couple of examples. Have you ever had a mate drink? This is what I've seen happen when people try mate for the first time with a straw and a gourd.

You will likely hold it in your hands, a bit unsure of how to grab it.

You'll feel its weight, the texture and colors of the gourd.

There's a rush all around you as you try to anticipate your reaction to it, and the questions start: *How does it taste like?* You hesitate, intrigued, staring at this strange, eclectic thing. *Do I try it? Will I even like it?*

You lower your head a bit, close your eyes, and breathe it in, earthy, rich, unfamiliar.

Then, you take the leap.

That first sip is an experience. Hesitation, curiosity, and then the bold plunge. The taste hits your tongue, unexpected yet oddly grounding. It's not just a drink; it's a ritual, a rite of passage.

Now, you can take a second sip, this time, without that rush of uncertainty. Without the gap between expectation and reality. Because now, the word 'mate' has the experience to anchor it.

A friend visited me the other day, telling me how fantastic it felt to be diagnosed with ADHD. Not that she liked the diagnosis itself, but because for years, she had felt off. Like something was happening to her, but she couldn't point at it. The moment she got a label? Bam! Now she is able to think about it, manage it, share it.

That is sensory experience moving to another level, the level of communication as she can now identify, recognize and label what she feels. That is the power of the signifier and the signified working together, intertwining inward and outward, internal and external worlds.

Until we have the words to hold an experience, it can feel like we are grasping at smoke. But once it's named, we can work with it, we can make sense of it. Once we reach that level, we can own it.

The same happens with the word 'love.' It's a concept until it's embodied. The scent of Jay Whozit's skin, the sound of their laugh echoing in your chest, the way your heartbeat syncs with Jay's in the stillness, the magnetic pull that makes you lean in, even when you know better.

That gives you a hint of what happens when all you have lived, fantasized, dreamed, craved and created with Jay Whozit falls apart after betrayal. And just like that, every memory, every shared moment with Jay Whozit is no longer a foundation; it's a question mark, hanging heavy over everything you once believed.

The signifier and signified spin together like a Möbius strip. A constant loop where meanings don't just happen once. They are redefined, twisted, reinterpreted over and over, not only along the timeline[13] of your life but also between your inner and outer world, who you are and what is happening around you.

I've seen it over and over in patients after a car accident, and just as often after a deep betrayal. They feel stuck in nowhere's land. As if the tools to make sense of their life have gone missing. They knew they were going somewhere... and then lost the track.

Here's what I tell them:

You've been dropped.

Not gently.

Not somewhere safe.

You've fallen into a deep hole -beyond time and space. And without a past, you can't project a future.

I've seen foreigners stay in the U.S. long after the reason they came is gone after being betrayed. Not because they want to stay, but because they feel stuck in space. Suspended. And ashamed.

Language is what you lean on to think, dream, wish, and connect. Then betrayal hits, and it all collapses.

---

[13] This is also called *après-coup*, a term in French psychoanalysis that means we see things differently in hindsight, after a second experience sheds new light on the first.

Suddenly, you can barely think. You don't know what's true anymore. The ground disappears.

The rules you lived by? Wiped out.

For a while, you can't do much of anything.

Trust yourself? Forget it.

You are raw emotion, without the capacity to think or act.

The signifier and signified spin with the Möbius[14] strip of space and the après-coup[15] of time. These are the tools your psyche uses to hold life together, emotionally, symbolically. But when betrayal hits, those systems crack. The power of your symbolic order falls apart. Your psyche can no longer weave meaning, process emotion, reality, ideas, or even memory with the same ease.

---

[14] In reference to the spacial line. Take a strip of paper, twist it, and join it into a loop (like an 8) with no clear inside or outside. That's the Möbius loop, a way to explain how our mind works. Desire, our sense of self and identity, the social and personal worlds constantly flow into and shape each other.

[15] In reference to the temporal line. Have you ever had an aha moment, when something from your past suddenly makes sense? That's how the present reshapes the past, giving it new meaning. At the same time, your past shapes how you see today (e.g. your coffee), and together they influence your future and vice versa. Because time is not linear. Après-coup is a French Psychoanalytic School that explains how these temporal instances constantly flow into and affect each other.

When what once were your most reliable anchors, the signifiers, go into free fall.. most things become questionable. And you are left on the edge, staring at a dubious past, stranded in a present that feels like someone else's life.

You want to move forward, but the future? It's impossible to picture it. Like staring into fog with no path ahead.

So, this is not only about what Jay Whozit did.

Betrayal is mainly about what it does to you.

Buckle up, this might sound heavy, but it is not the end of the story. Let's keep cracking the code.

The ego emerges as a semiotic representation, built from reflective mirroring and supportive life experiences. Severe betrayal dismantles that representation.

I will say it again, the ego is a representation, an idea, built from the reflections we get from others and the experiences that shape us. It's the story we tell ourselves about who we are.

Severe betrayal doesn't just shake that story. It tears it apart, leaving you questioning everything you thought was true about yourself.

Get this, betrayal stands apart from a traumatic diagnosis like posttraumatic stress disorder (PTSD) or Complex-PTSD, even if you were stamped with that label. Betrayal crashes into your ego, while PTSD is about facing a threat to your life. One shakes your body to its core. The other tears down your identity, your self-narrative, the very essence of who you feel you are.

Trauma means 'wound' in Greek. PTSD is a life-threatening event that wounds your narcissism, the very space that homes your ego. Betrayal, on the other hand, wounds the representation itself, or its source. Because the ego isn't just a construct. It is a representation that is embodied[16]. The symptoms may look alike, but recognizing this distinction is crucial for treatment.

Just remember: Empowerment isn't about forcing your will on others or bulldozing through life with sheer force against those around you. It's about feeling grounded in who you are, comfortable in your skin, clear-headed, and steady even when the world around you shakes.

Empowerment is that quiet confidence that lets you move with purpose, trusting you can handle whatever comes your way without losing yourself in the process.

And life?

---

[16] Representation (betrayal) / Embodied (PTSD)

Life is about finding your mojo, your woo, not running to the nearest cave. Isolation doesn't protect you; it only sharpens the knife of self-betrayal.

When the rug gets pulled out from under you, nothing makes sense anymore. That sign called Jay -your partner, your lighthouse of safety- disintegrates... Now it has a question mark next to it, and nothing feels steady enough to put the pieces back together.

So, we can say betrayal is broken trust.

Or we can admit that betrayal is when...

-***Your sense of self shatters,*** but only for an instant, as if you are staring into the abyss, wondering if you'll ever stand tall again. Hear this: like the phoenix, you will rise. The comeback is already written in your bones.

-***And you are left utterly disempowered,*** stripped of your sense of agency and capacity to think, decide and act with purpose. But that part? That's temporary too. Trust me, I've been there.

Do you know when betrayal happens? Many times, I believe, it happens when a part of us is secretly ready for it, and we would sprint a thousand miles to avoid the disintegration that follows.

So, here's what I want you to remember: Even when the foundation cracks and the whole structure shakes, it's not the end. Like a forest fire, the burning clears the way for new growth, fertilizing the ground for something stronger to take root.

That's the hidden magic of betrayal: it strips you bare, but in doing so, it reveals something you didn't realize you've had all along. Since birth, we are wired to depend, to seek comfort and validation from others. But betrayal cracks that foundation, forcing you to face what's been beneath it this whole time: YOU!

It's the moment you realize you are not just reacting to life, you are shaping it. You are not just someone to be held or seen. The world doesn't just happen to you: you are a builder, laying down each brick with intention. You are the one holding the brush, painting the canvas

As the smoke clears, you feel it: steady, quiet, undeniable. The power to make things happen was always yours. Only now you are beginning to see it for the first time.

6- Jekyll & Hyde

Can I spill a bit more theory really quick?

As I said before, from the moment you popped into this world, your body's been a top-tier sensor, picking up signals faster than your mind can even go, 'Wait, what?'

Perception? It's your body grabbing the world's signals and flipping them into electrical impulses that zip through your nervous system.

Those signals don't just sit there. They fire up hormones, stirring emotions and sparking reactions. That's why every time you touch, taste, smell, or feel something, it's not just a surface-level vibe. Oh no, it digs deep, flooding your system with oxytocin, adrenaline, endorphins... whatever the moment calls for.

That sensory info gets processed, stored as learned experience, and baked into your neural pathways, creating a database you don't even know you are constantly tapping into.

Next time? When you lock eyes with something or someone, it's like a déjà vu with a twist. Your brain lights up, connecting that moment to a leftover vibe from within. It's a heatwave of familiarity that flavors reality, making it feel deliciously personal, charged by everything you've already lived that comes to mind.

That is sensory, emotion, and know-how tag-teaming across your past, present, and future.

Let's revisit a basic act of life: how do you take your coffee? You have tried it before (past), so now you know exactly how you like it.

More than that, on a freezing day you can even see the steam swirling up, feel the warmth radiating from the cup's edges as you wrap your hands around it and take that first, blissful sip, all that before you have stepped into the coffee shop.

Do you know how that happens? That magic is provided by your body firing up those old neural pathways created from having had a hot cup of coffee before.

Mixing know-how with emotion? That brings back the rush of indulging in what you crave, and helping you taste it way before you arrive at the coffee shop.

Being with Jay? That follows the same damn pattern.

Just as I told you on *Cracking the Code of Betrayal*.. You know where your partner fits in the big picture, when Jay is at work, with friends, etc. The general concept of what it is to be Jay Whozit as an individual, the signified.

Yet *your* body has been basically Sherlock Holmes since the day you two met, picking up on every clue of sensory data. Jay's soft voice, the sideways glance, that unique smile, and a personal scent so uniquely *Jay*... *you* name it. All those little cues you've been treasuring come together to form the signifier. When you talk about Jay, your words are not general. They are funded on all those things, and on how you see, feel, and envision your being with Jay.

All that is personal. That's private. That is your unique way of relating to Jay, something that can't be shared or truly felt by anyone else. You can describe it, sure, but no one will feel it the way you do. In a sense, it's how Jay anchors in your body, from all the experiences and those neural pathways you created from being with J.W.

Now, when all those clues line up, when Jay's actions match your expectations: Bam! That's when the magic kicks in, and you start building trust.

What happens then? Then, trust builds hope.

What does that really mean? It means you've gathered enough information on the way Jay embodies Jay that even if you saw them from afar, and without wearing your glasses, you'd still recognize whether it was Jay or not. Your senses just know.

Even more, you have seen and feel enough of Jay to put in place some solid expectations. You are not merely guessing, whether it will show up on time or not, if Jay is allergic to nuts, eats burgers with ketchup, or gets a thrill with horror movies... You are in the *knowing*.

So, when you first met Jay Whozit, this individual was barely that: a Whozit. A "Who's this?" But then, you started sharing moments, conversations, late-night texts, movie marathons, laughs, and even those heavier talks. ..and guess what? You began to crack the code of what makes Jay tick. More importantly, you started to figure out why you like being around this fascinating new person.

Pretty soon, Jay Whozit turned into "my friend Jay," or J.W. if we are feeling cute. The friend who makes you feel like you are on top of the world when you are out grabbing food or hitting up the movies. That's Jay, the one who makes the regular stuff feel super special.

And let's get real for a second: Jay didn't just bring the good energy; Jay added a whole new layer to you.

Suddenly, there are things you enjoy more with Jay than with anyone else. Jay makes you shiver with excitement like nobody else. It ups your game.

...And that right there? That's how trust starts.

It sneaks up on you, built on those little things you internalize and stash away in your own personal memory vault. It's more than trust. It is trust supercharged with hope, loaded with expectations, and drenched in all the right chemistry.

Can you tell me what really means to *know* something? Well, it means you stop noticing what's right in front of you, unless it annoys you enough to grab your attention.

At some point, it simply feels so good to be close to Jay that, whether you realize it or not, you pump up the good parts while sweeping the red flags right under the rug.

You crave that person. You love who you are when you are with Jay, and before you know it, you dream up all the future plans, maybe even dropping hints about marriage.

You forgive those excuses when Jay falls short. You still see J.W. as reliable, even when things don't quite add up. If someone tries to throw shade or spill some tea about Jay, you brush it off because, hey, you are the closest to this person, correct? Then, logical conclusion: You know Jay best.

Get this: that only works... until it doesn't.

When betrayal hits deep, it feels like everything is collapsing. You are consumed by rage, struggling to hold onto your integrity in the midst of a seismic shift that wrecks your sense of self.

Think about it. You built up this perfect picture in your mind, adding every little moment to the canvas. That image, full with sensory info about what Jay is to you, how it feels to be the lucky one. It became your "together against the odds" rallying cry into the future.

Eventually, things start to shift, don't they? Suddenly, you are stepping into quarrels without even knowing what you did wrong.

The sly criticism chips away your wings. You realize you used to have friends, but somehow, your whole world has shrunk to no more than Jay and the kids. Ugh… and when the kids are around? Oh, it's like Jay is bothered. Jealous of anything that steals your attention away.

After forgiving excuses and brushing off all sorts of alarms, at one point and beyond your willingness to go through this.. questions start creeping in.

'*Where is the person I thought I married?*'

…And that's when it hits you. All those little things that didn't quite fit with your idea of the loving Jay, all those gut messages, those silent bugs in your stomach, the neck pains, the shivers. You tucked them away, neatly silencing them one by one.

Your inner detective kept waving at you, warning you of Dr. Jekyll morphing into Mr. Hyde. Even then, you kept working overtime to keep it all together, pushing forward no matter what.

Here's the thing, though: when you keep moving forward while ignoring reality, you start stepping into fantasy territory. And that, my friend, as I told you before, is dangerous ground.

Because that only works until it no longer does.

Self-betrayal happens way before betrayal ever does. You know when? When you told your therapist that something was off, but you failed to listen to yourself. When your therapist tried to warn you about the stone in the road, and you chose to close your eyes instead[17].

Take Robert, for instance. He was in love with his new wife until one day, she decided to stop taking her bipolar medication. The irritability grew into aggression. He wasn't sure where he stood anymore. Did she still love him? Did she hate him? One day, he realized she

---

[17] This isn't just about treatment compliance, but also about recognizing that non-prescribed or recreational drugs are often laced, and can increase the risk of dysfunction and violence.

couldn't stop. She became loud, disappeared for days, hated everything, including herself.

Then, just as suddenly, she decided to go back to treatment. The frenzy faded, and there she was again: Dr. Jekyll. Loving, stable, promising that this time, she would never stop taking her medication.

...And Robert?

He believed her.

Not only because he loved her, but because it was convenient. Because if she was back, he didn't have to figure out what all that meant to him. He didn't have to face the truth his therapist had tried to tell him, that treatment noncompliance in bipolar disorder isn't the exception. It's the rule.[18]

Since betrayal begins with self-betrayal, I believe a part of us always knows what's truly happening. What is unfolding beneath the surface, in that hidden,

---

[18] Skipping meds in bipolar disorder is more common than not. This isn't failure, it's reality. People stop for many reasons, and recognizing these patterns is key. Expect it, plan for it, and don't let it catch you off guard. I've worked with many patients who struggle with this, sometimes in ways they don't expect: seasonal changes, vacations, even small disruptions can throw things off. The real challenge isn't just compliance vs. noncompliance… The real challenge is stability vs. destabilization. Instead of aiming for perfection, try maintaining balance when dysregulation pulls you off course. Dysfunction isn't always loud; sometimes, it's subtle. What matters is having a plan to navigate the turbulence without losing control.

underground reality. We are just not ready to face the truth. At the moment, we rather compromise. Opting for situational decisions over the big picture, we rather sprint, shut the door, close our eyes and hope for the best.

When betrayal finally strikes, your world doesn't solely crack on the outside. It smashes right into that inner world you have so carefully crafted through the years. It brings it all down. Your past. Your present. Your future.

When someone turns against you, it feels like a part of you turns against you, too. You start doubting your own instincts, questioning whether the warning signs were ever real, or if you just made it all up. That's the real gut-punch. You are free-falling with no bottom end in sight.

Severe betrayal is not an event, but an experience. When everything you believed about someone who mattered deeply shatters... and in that wreckage, your own sense of self is destroyed.

It's not about them.

It's not about what happened.

It's all about how that affected your sense of self.

Because at certain moments in life, something strikes us so deeply it rewires how we make sense of the world and how we connect with it, our very essence of joy, our *jouissance*[19]. Betrayal is one of those moments.

At that very second when you feel the rug ripping beneath you, and everything you swept underneath comes tumbling out... you are left free-diving into this abyss of truth, crashing right into your sense of self. You are stuck in a present where the past is burst meaningless, as nothing makes sense anymore. And the future? It's impossible to picture.

Severe betrayal is far more than breaking trust.

It breaks you and leaves you disempowered.

When you hit rock bottom, it cuts so deep it carves away the layers of your felt identity. You are left sifting through the wreckage of who you thought you were, the beliefs you held, and what your life once was. As if you were not human anymore. Worse yet, it steals your power to act, to steer your own life. That sense of agency? Gone.

---

[19] The *jouissance* is often considered a tug-of-war between hurt and pleasure. More than just that, the *jouissance* shapes the way we engage with life's mix of joy and struggle. It's not just about *what* we pursue but *how* we pursue it, even when it leads us to the edge of discomfort. *Jouissance* is the fire that drives us forward, often into places where satisfaction feels just out of reach, even as we stumble. It shapes our stance, our drive, and how we keep moving through the messiness of life.

You might even have no capacity to think about any of this for a while. It's okay to stay there for a bit. Don't make it too long, though.

Allow yourself to weep, which is like crying but without the clarity of emotions or the certainty of knowing exactly why you cry. No tidy answers. Just pure, unfiltered release.

Your body starts healing before your mind even knows what's happening. That's how it goes, your body always kicks off the healing before your brain catches up. Little by little, you will start piecing together who you are again. It's a process, so give it time.

Help it along by taking those simple walks with your pet and, above all, be patient with yourself. Healing doesn't follow a straight line. It moves in waves and stages.

Of course, there's the anger. When the shock wears off? Oh, you'll be *pissed*... and it's okay to be angry for a while. t's perfectly fine to be angry for a while. But don't let it consume you, turning you into someone you are not. No way. Let that anger light you up, not drag you down.

Let that anger fuel the fire to rebuild stronger, smarter, and more unstoppable than before. Channel that fire into your comeback. Now it's time to show the world -and yourself- exactly who you are. This isn't about bouncing back. This is a full-blown revolution of self. So go ahead, show them what you are made of.

7- From Cloud Nine to Real Grind

Stop that movie for a second... Do you remember the day you first met Jay Whozit?

Come closer... yes, yes, right here.

Want to take a little peek? Take a look with my super imaginary magnifier.

Here's what went down: your heart skipped a beat, your mind was racing, and your whole body felt... off. Not in a bad way, though. More like you were pleasantly bothered by a stream of energy.

Something was different, wasn't it?

Remember? You felt like floating in cloud number nine.

In search for unwavering love, you have started by putting Jay on a pedestal, haven't you? Making Jay larger than life, brighter, more important, more everything than you could ever be. And just like that, the spotlight is turned one and you began playing your part... The Fixer, the Martyr, or some other role, each a survival script in the theater of love, designed to keep them glowing while you dimmed yourself down.

After that move, one of two things happens: either you have found someone who thrives on that pedestal and settles into the role with ease, or you have stumbled upon someone who is willing to show their own shortcomings, as you secretly hope to.

Now, if your partner fits that first mold, buckle up: they're likely to be a narcissist. They flourish on that pedestal, soaking up gaze, praise, feeding off on your need for them to be bigger than life.

...and you?

Well, it can be awesome at first. Yet, loving this person will slowly drain you, as it probably already has. They won't meet you halfway. They are more likely to cross their arms, like it's "your" problem.

Love? That's not mutually exchanged. It's a performance, and you are the lead actor in a script you never agreed to.

Your time, energy, and sense of self? Tributes to your partner's feeling of grandiosity.

Your job? To orbit around this person. Ready to serve, ready to please.

Anticipate their needs before they even speak them. Be endlessly available, while they remain selectively present. They bask in the glow of admiration, while you exhaust yourself keeping the pedestal polished and steady.

...And if you dare to step back?

Expect guilt trips, silent treatments, or a well-timed charm offensive to pull you right back into place.

On the Other Hand...

I am keeping my fingers cross hoping you landed a healthy one. They are someone who is willing to be open, and real.

Did you? Great, good for you.

Now, two things can happen:

Either you are both working on it and enjoying what you are building together, or despite the best intentions, the whole thing has gone a little ...rotten.

When it's good, it's *really* good but based in reality.

You know that kind of good? It is going really, really good for you?

That "really, really good" sounds a bit too much to me. But you are telling me that your relationship is based in reality ...? That there are low moments along the way. Yet, there is honesty, and the kind of trust that makes you feel like you are building something real...?

Well, get this: when the illusion of idealization wears off and things start to sour, it can turn wild fast.

Expectations pile up.

Insecurities creep in.

Old traumas wake up.

And suddenly, that openness you admired starts to feel fragile... maybe even draining.

What? That's where you are at now?! ...Oh. So you are the one with the resolution to love unapologetically? To take on the full challenge –and all its frustrations– of figuring out how to love your partner on their terms.

Patient.

Exhausted.

Second-guessing yourself.

Walking on eggshells.

Working overtime to make your lover happy...

Feeling responsible for every shortcoming, every mood shift, every moment that doesn't go right.

Wishing and praying for just one more good day.

And still, you are not even good at it.

Because no matter how much you adjust, anticipate, accommodate, it's never enough.

The bar keeps moving, and you keep running. Hoping that if you just try harder, love will finally settle into something safe. Something solid.

I'm sorry, but when the exhilaration fades, the romance that once felt magical...?

It starts feeling more like a contract.

Terms...

Conditions...

Emotional fine print.

Genuine kindness? Replaced by policies, power plays and an erratic behavior you failed to see.

And love? You can barely find it anymore. It's buried beneath all the silent rules and impossible expectations you hold for each other.

I know it's exhausting.

What I don't know is... *How do you keep doing it?*

What you called love? That wasn't love. That was...

Acceleration.

Fantasy.

A dopamine-fueled thrill ride you mistook for connection.

You didn't fall in love. You slid into chaos with a smile, hoping the speed would hide the cracks. But love doesn't feel like this. Love isn't a cardio workout. It's a steady hand, no whiplash included.

You are trudging through your partner's fears, old wounds, and that deep, relentless pull to merge into you –fusing together in a desperate attempt to silence the anxious whisper that tells them you might leave.

...while making you believe it's your job to secure the relationship to keep them from walking away.

Have you stopped to think that when you are the one doing the work, holding it all together, while they test the limits...

...the balance is off?

And it's draining you both.

Either way, you are at a crossroads:

Stay present and keep trying to build that connection, or watch it slip through your fingers.

And if you've ever been singled out as the one who

"doesn't care,"

"doesn't listen,"

"always falls short"...

...and you are left thinking, What? When?

Hear me out: You are responsible for your actions, but you are not responsible for other people's feelings: That's their end of the stick.

So next time, instead of spiraling into how you supposedly failed...

Hit pause.

Step back.

Say you are thirsty, but let them know you care and want to hear them out.

Validate[20] their side, then go grab a cup of iced water. That buys you both five minutes.

....And just so we are clear, validating isn't the same as agreeing. You are showing interest, not co-signing to their version of the story.

Now, sit down somewhere comfortable and get curious about what they feel, and don't take it personal. In Binary Relationship Theory, this isn't about you. It's about how they perceive the relationship. The link, the connection. It might even be laced with old projections.

So don't get defensive.

---

[20] That validation? It's a lifeline for anyone with abandonment wounds. Add a "Just grabbing a cup of water," and you are not just leaving, you are signaling safety. Did you say you are coming back? Mean it ...or earn a bad rap.

Don’t take it personally.

Listen, not to who they say you are, but to how they feel in the relationship.

Unconditional Love?

The reality is that love isn't a static thing. It bends, shifts, and sometimes struggles are part of the deal. But what happens when the version of love you long for doesn’t match the reality of the person in front of you?

Bring that magnifier back for a second. I’m about to show you something that’s been right in front of your eyes this whole time, so close, it probably hasn’t even sunk in yet.

Take a look at this third option...

Do you know what happens when your partner doesn’t live up to that bloody pedestal? The one you built by projecting all your hopes onto them while ignoring the parts that didn’t quite fit. When you’ve made your lover larger than life to keep it all running smoothly?

When the early vibe of idealization wears off, endless devotion turns out to be loaded with demands. Yes, your craving for unconditional love and your desire to make them more than they are, can backfire.

Are you sure that you didn't end up wounding this healthy one you got?

Because, sure, you are great at demanding unconditionality.

Now, how good are you at giving it?

Nope, this is not the fairytale you envisioned. Instead, it morphs into a game of trials and tests that leaves your partner confused and drained by a love that had conditions after all:

'If you loved me, you'd do this...'

'If I mattered, you'd answer every call and all the texts I sent this morning,'

'If you really cared, you'd prove it.'

That push-and-pull? It's really you swinging between confidence and a deep, gnawing fear of rejection. You are afraid you are not enough, or worse, that the love will vanish.

While you are caught up in that emotional rollercoaster, your partner is left clinging on, hurt, confused and trying to decode and navigate your anxious tug-of-war.

Unconditional love? Yes, sure.

You forgot that love is a give, not a take. Instead, you pile on expectations, set up tests and challenges, and try to control the very thing you are scared of losing.

Otherwise, you withdraw. Not because you don't care, but because you are exhausted. You feel guilty, afraid you have already messed things up so badly that the connection is broken to the point of no return.

Then, what do you do? You pull away, convincing yourself that abandoning ship is safer than being abandoned.

...Have you consider that when you are constantly retreating, afraid of what might happen and refusing even a moment of vulnerability, you are not just breaking the link, you are cutting off the very chance of fixing it?

You are so caught up in the fear of being left that you forget that love, real love, is fiery and risky. It's about staying when it's hard, not running at the first sign of trouble. Specially when so many of those moments of 'trouble' are misinterpretations, mixed signals, or fantasy colliding with reality.

People think dodging suffering will keep them safe.

I hear it constantly, folks jumping into coaching, trying to spare others from pain like that is the answer.

Here is a thought: avoiding pain doesn't get you anywhere new. It just leaves you circling the same old track, stuck.

So, grab that pain, break it open, and let it light a fire under you. Look at it from every angle. Let it fuel you into the next stage, pushing you past survival into full-on living.

When fear has you by the throat, stepping back can feel safer than risking the hurt.

Here is the reality you need to consider: you are choosing the safety of distance over the vulnerability of truly being loved.

When you do that, love doesn't stand a chance.

Because while you are trying to protect your heart, you are building walls and putting up more obstacles than you realize.

It's not love slipping through your fingers: it's life.

The fullness of it, the possibilities, and all the experiences you were too afraid to have.

Vulnerability is that edge between you and possibility, a place buzzing with butterflies, part joy, part fright. Hold onto hope's joy, step out with determination, and let love grow wild and free.

That is where life happens.

Because sometimes the safe zone is the dead zone.

In the end? It is only you standing in the way of what you crave.

Either way, pure acceptance is not what it seems. It's not about placing someone above yourself, demanding more than they can give or tiptoeing around our partner's shifting expectations. It's about meeting them where they are, with all the risks and imperfections that come with it ...so long these are livable.

We all do it. We all start by placing our Jay Whozit up on a pedestal, wishing they will lift us with that boundless passion we've craved since we were infants.

Yes, since that time!

Do you know where that comes from? We've been seeking it since the very moment we land on earth, fresh out of the womb and right into mom's comforting arms. That's the instant we grab onto life for the very first time, and works like an imprint that pushes us to search for comfort and security all over again.

Hear me out.

I hate to break it to you, but someone has to bring you down from that fairytale: love is never unconditional.

Even the affection we think of as purest, parental care, comes with its terms. Why? Because real love, true love, is not about endless cuddles and no-strings attached devotion to a baby. It's about protection, guidance, and the not so sexy work of shaping you into someone who is ready to take on the world.

As grown-ups, we put conditions on our affairs all the time. Whether it's faithfulness, honesty, money, and all sorts of things. Affections thrives because of these agreements. Mutual respect is essential.

Do you still rather seek unconditional love?

Then get this: What you are really looking for is a safety net, a guarantee that you can give as little as you want and still get everything in return.

That's not love.

That is control. You want love without the risk of not being loved back, and that's not how it works. Love isn't a leash. It's a dance.

So, wake up! Let go of the need to control love, and feel free to choose it authentically, knowing it's a two-way street that starts with self-love. Before setting any expectations in relationships, you need to know who you are, where you are headed, and respect your own needs and identity.

The real strength in any relationship doesn't come from control or boundaries. It's about feeling at home in your own world, let it fill you up from the inside. About knowing, trusting, and anchoring yourself so deeply that you can be fully open without losing who you are, without that lurking fear of rejection.

When you have that inner compass, you are not holding back or putting up walls. You are grounded enough to let people in while keeping yourself whole.

You can't make someone care for you on your terms or bend them to your rhythm. All you can do is work on your own steps, and invite others into the dance. Only when you feel at home in you, you can step into someone else's space as your true self, open and ready to take that journey together. Explore if the tune feels right. See where the music takes you.

The trick is in letting go of the need to own love or make it bulletproof. Because real love might be messy, but that is the beauty of it: two imperfect people, choosing each other again and again.

The beauty is in what you create together, the third element that holds you both, steady and wild. It's this bond that lets you be fully yourself, creating something bigger than either of you alone.

You have got to keep dancing, because love is always moving, always evolving. You cannot keep it on lockdown.

A balanced partnership is about respect and genuine connection. Solid enough to keep you grounded, yet flexible enough to let you fly. That's the magic that empowers you to face the tough calls, anchored yet open, ready for whatever is next.

8- Time Out: Gotta Think This Through

So here you are, stuck between what you feel and what you refuse to admit. You've been brushing off that slow burning discomfort, telling yourself it's just a phase, just stress, just your imagination. But deep down, you know better.

When a relationship starts eating away at your peace, when the connection that once felt like home now feels like a slow suffocation, you owe it to yourself to stop and think.

Really think.

Like connect the dots between heart, gut, and brain type of thinking.

Because when you are excusing disrespect, clinging to resentment, or numbing yourself just to get through the days, it is time to ask yourself:

What exactly are you fighting for?

A love that strengthens you, or a habit that's wearing you down?

This isn't about making snap decisions. It's about getting brutally honest with yourself before you end up so lost that you don't even recognize the person in the mirror.

If your relationship feels more like a slow, painful drain than something that fuels you, it's time to hit pause. No more sugarcoating, no more justifications. Just you, facing the raw truth: what are you really holding on to, and at what cost?

This isn't about quick exits or easy answers. It's about getting real with yourself and figuring out what actually makes you whole. Check if you recognize yourself and your partner in any of these traits:

Disrespect becomes normal: If you are being disrespected, that is a bloody sign that you have given up your self-worth, and that you are not expecting anything better. If you are the one being disrespectful, it reveals just how little you value your partner.

Constant resentment: This is darn toxic & draining. Stop holding onto anger or constantly thinking about what happened.

Emotional numbness: ...So you've become rotten, disconnected, and blasted indifferent?

Loss of Self: You have lost sight of who you are and what you damn well deserve.

If any and most of these patterns got a *yes I do*, then.. what on earth are you bloody doing with your life? ..and let's be clear, I'm not even going to entertain the issues of abuse, unhealthy compromise, or dependency.

When trust is broken and disrespect stunts your blasted growth, drop the freakin' urge to fix the unfixable!

...you are not a full-time caregiver in a one-sided emotional hospice.

9- Unclench, Babe

You've taken a step back. You've asked yourself the hard questions. Maybe you've even admitted that something feels… off. And now, here comes the part most of us dread. The moment where your gut starts whispering (or screaming) that things aren't adding up.

Ever had that feeling? Riding high on the thrill of love, then suddenly spiraling into all types of flashing alarms your intuition's been throwing at you? Feeling torn between the addictive rush of being with Jay and the gut-wrenching anxiety of your instincts blaring alarms?

And what do you do when you get to this point? When your intuition is throwing out warning signs like it's on fire? Instead of trusting it, you start second-guessing yourself, searching for excuses, trying to quiet that nagging voice inside.

Not anymore. It's time to unclench, babe. Time to stop gaslighting yourself and start listening to the signals your body, your instincts, and all those tiny, barely noticeable shifts are trying to tell you. Because when something is off, believe me… it usually is.

Before we learned to label things with words and logic, we have that inner radar based on sensory info. That's your intuition in action. Picking up on gestures, emotions, and all those subtle things that might otherwise go unnoticed.

Raw, unfiltered, and often more accurate than you think, your gut alerts you to shifts and dangers.

When your partner starts acting shady, your gut will be the first to notice it. But here's what usually happens: most people waste time having long debates between their gut, their mind, and their heart. They would rather sit with acid reflux than admit their gut was screaming truth at them.

Betrayal, deceit, infidelity, isn't always obvious. It's sneaky, slippery, and packed with little clues patiently waiting for us to be brave enough to uncovered them.

Don't worry, you are not going to wander through this mystery alone. I'm about to give you the playbook. The juicy, tell-all list of red flags that scream 'something's up!'

Whether it's the sudden obsession with their phone or that new gym routine that came out of nowhere, these cues are your backstage pass to uncovering the truth.

The common threat is this: spot out those spicy shifts in your partner's behavior. Regardless of where or what, something is off.

Hiding Gaze: Those eyes that once couldn't get enough of you now seem to dodge your gaze? Yeah, something's definitely up.

New "Private" Mode: Suddenly, your partner locks their phone and guards the passcode like it's Fort Knox. Does it feel more like they are locking *you* out of it? Sure, everyone deserves privacy, but when secrecy pops up out of nowhere, it begs a question: *What changed?*

Hot and Cold Routine: The bedroom energy shifts drastically. Your partner suddenly gets overly passionate, starts treating cuddling like a chore, or worse, picks a fight just to dodge intimacy altogether.

The Cheerleader Switch-Up: Unexpectedly, your partner can't get enough of you working late, taking on new projects, or just being out of their side... I mean, the house. That's when you start wondering, *Since when did I get such an eager supportive?* Yeah, there could be a reason.

Glow-Up: A sudden interest in their appearance. New clothes, a different perfume, hitting the gym like it's their new job. Shopping sprees and style upgrades out of nowhere? It hits you with this question: *Who exactly are you trying to impress?*

Guilt Gifts: You are showered with gifts and attention, *just because*. It feels like a dream... until an unspoken weight creeps in behind every "just because." It's almost like they are overcompensating, but for what? No reason is ever given.

Changed Playlists: Their music tastes start to shift toward genres they never cared for. Is it a newfound hobby, or is there someone else's influence?

Social Media Switch-Up: They are glued to the screen, grinning at messages, and let's face it, it's not you making them smile. Those late-night buzzes? Oh, they're screaming things words can't even touch. What's happening behind that digital curtain?

The Vanishing Act: They become Houdini when it comes to their whereabouts, more business trips, new project requiring late nights at work, or vague explanations that don't quite add up.

Defensive Diva: When you casually ask about their day or plans, and suddenly, they get all defensive? Oh, dear, that's you unknowingly hitting a nerve you didn't even know was there. Innocent question, *guilty reaction*.

"Just Friends": The sudden appearance of a "close friend" they have never mentioned before. They insist it's platonic, but the energy says otherwise.

Trouble sleeping?: Been pushing aside that gnawing feeling in your stomach? Those 3 a.m. wake-up calls? Yeah, that's your gut screaming, trying to grab your attention any way it can. Piecing together what your brain's been too scared to face. Don't sleep on it, most of the times, your gut knows when something's off.

10 - The Real Scandal? Tearing Apart Your Whole Damn Universe

Betrayal hits like that last drop spilling over the cup. You see the little things that don't add up, but you keep pushing through... until suddenly, something breaks and you can't take it anymore.

When you get to this point, you crack wide open... as if the whole world around you imploded into tiny pieces. Everything falls apart. Nothing makes sense anymore and the only thing that remains standing is your shock.

The very intimacy that binds us also makes us vulnerable. Our closest relationships are woven from layers of shared experiences, trust, and the belief that those closest to us not only understand us deeply but care for our well-being.

By choosing to witness our existence, they give us purpose and breathe life into our sense of self. This sacred connection is what makes these bonds so vital, and so fragile.

Our soulmates complete and complement us. They are our 'better half.' We see our partners as reflections of ourselves, kindred spirits we believe will uphold our deepest values. More than that, we project our best traits onto those we love, elevating them above the rest. But when betrayal hits, it wipes out that illusion in an instant.

When we think of 'betrayal,' most people picture broken trust or confidence. In 2014, Leeker and Carlozzi framed infidelity as "a violation of the ground rules established by the couple regarding emotional and sexual involvement with third parties." It makes you wonder...

Is cheating really about breaking a rule?

...is it the act itself what shakes us to our core? If so, what part of it?

...And why does infidelity seem to get the spotlight when we talk about betrayal, as if it's the only way to be hurt? Sure, cheating hits hard, but betrayal comes in many forms -lies, deceit, broken promises, or even indifference. It's not the *how* that cuts the deepest. It's the feeling of being blindsided by someone we trusted.

Even more mind-bubbling, why have we neatly boxed infidelity into "sex"? We both know this cuts way deeper than who's sleeping with whom.

When you have poured your heart, time, and energy into a relationship, it's not the physical act that astonishes you. It's that, in addition to all that, what hurts the most is how betrayal makes you feel: completely invalidated. Like your entire existence in the relationship has been tossed aside... and you are not sure since when. You feel violated to the core, an absolute idiot in a movie you didn't even sign up for.

Of course, cheating is a major part of it.

Yet what truly defines infidelity as betrayal isn't the reason for breaking the bond. Not a breaking of trust as everybody says. But the aftermath of destruction:

If you are left feeling crushed, no longer knowing who the heck you are...

If you are also left disempowered, adrift in an ocean of nothingness...

When the world you built together -the universe you held up with quiet effort and daily giving- lies shattered, pieces scattered all around you, what's really happening is that betrayal becomes the loss of you.

After you realize you were building castles in the air, and everything falls apart, you'll go through a transformation, peeling away the layers that once defined you.

You'll stop trusting

Feel ashamed.

...and watch your world crumble.

Your mind races, desperate to piece together the puzzle: when did it begin, what was your role, how did it all unravel? Memories flood in, dissecting the subtle changes: was the switch in aftershave or perfume a clue? Those late nights "at the office": were they real, or just another layer of deceit? The fireworks the last time you had sex: was that passion real, or was it out of guilt? That trip we took: was it to be with me, or to escape?

....And hauntingly, you try to recall the last time your partner could look you straight in the eye, with genuine honesty.

You are so angry, you don't know what to do. You try screaming, and surprisingly, you find that yelling at your kids' sports games is not only easier, it's even socially encouraged at times. Another reason not to miss any game.

Then, of course, there's the crying. The kind that sneaks up on you in the middle of nowhere, like when you are doing the dishes or stuck in traffic. You try to hold it together, but it spills out, uncontrollable and relentless.

The exhaustion, the heavy weight of depression, it's easier to hide away, wrapped in the comfort of a home.

You cut off, stop going out with friends and family, and you turn your home into a sanctuary in which only a seldom few are ever invited in.

It feels like being trapped in an emotional loop that won't stop. Each turn and dip forcing you to confront what's happening, while nothing feels solid anymore. The cycle is relentless, exhausting, and infuriating, as you try to piece together a reality that once seemed so certain.

When someone betrays you, they don't break the trust you had in them, they make you question trusting anyone, including yourself. It's like they have stomped all over your heart, leaving you drowning in shame, doubting your worth, and second-guessing the appropriateness of every decision any gesture.

Your sense of self is fragmented, and the power to act with certainty has blipped out of existence. Suddenly, you feel like you have lost control over everything you have built and the future you thought was yours... and that feeling? It stings like hell.

Betrayal leaves a mark that changes how you see yourself and the world around you. You misplace that inner sense of direction that once set you apart and guided you. As if someone had stripped away your independence and left you unsure of your own strength.

So, when your life becomes disorienting -like being a stranger in your own skin-, and you no longer know who you are, what you want, or what's worth fighting for. When the moments you once shared with your betrayer, once so certain, now carry a question mark. When even the clarity of your goals fades... that's the real betrayal: the loss of *you*..

I believe that's why so many relationships don't break apart right after cheating (between 60-80%, depending on the research)[21]. They fall prey of attachment ambivalence...

I want to confront you, but I'm afraid of pushing you away. What if I lose you completely?

I don't trust you anymore, but I can't live without you.

Am I being too harsh? Or maybe I'm not being harsh enough.

I'm so angry I could walk away forever. But I can't leave. I can't let go.

If I leave, I might regret it. But if I stay, what if nothing changes?

---

[21] 83% by Hollenbeck & Steffens, 2024.

You are trying so hard to make it up to me... but I don't know if I'll ever feel safe again.

Does it sound familiar? In this trial-and-error hustle between hurt and hope, many give the relationship another try. Why? Because once you lose yourself, you become dependent. It's like you hang on to the coattails of what's left, clinging to the very thing that broke you, hoping it'll somehow stick you back together.

The million-dollar question: Can it be fixed? Here's what I can tell you...

There are success stories.

There are stories that hold up for a while, then fall apart.

There are far too many stories of people stuck in cycles of betrayal, spinning the same wheel over and over.

...and yes, there are stories where the relationship was already crumbling. Infidelity was just the final push out the door.

Now, put this in your own words. Say it out loud. Listen to yourself.

Is your question really about "getting my life back"

...or is it about "getting our life back together?"

Connect your heart and your brain:

Where does the answer take you?

What does your body say?

I was talking to a friend about this book, and we got onto the topic of the nuclear family. I told her about my mother, how she never finished school because of severe asthma. As a child, she was told her husband would take care of her. But it's never just about finances, is it? It's more about the soft labor of existence, the choreography of the ordinary. Managing a home, calling for repairs, handling the little things that make up a life.

So, what now?

First, remember attachment theory's warning: once we form deep emotional bonds, they're stubborn. Even after betrayal, that bond tightens, like letting go would tear away a piece of you. It's not just the fear of losing them; it's the fear of losing yourself.

...Unless, of course, you've got an avoidant attachment style. But let's be real, that's not you. No, you are riding the rollercoaster of pain and comfort-seeking, mistaking that toxic cycle for love. And when you've lost your sense of self, it's so easy to confuse dependence with stability.

That's why so many stay, circling the same drain, clinging to any shred of self-worth they can salvage from the wreckage.

But here's the kicker: holding onto the past won't heal you. It keeps you trapped in frustration and pain. Sometimes the boldest, strongest move you can make is to stare down your losses and let them go. That's when healing starts, not when you glue the broken pieces back together, but when you clear the table and make space for the version of you that is ready to rise.

11- Running on Empty, Drowning in It All

Betrayal isn't a touch-and-go. It moves in, rearranges the furniture in your head, and overstays its welcome like a bad houseguest. Before you rise like a phoenix, you'll have to wade through the wreckage -bruised, exhausted, and questioning everything. The hyper-awareness? The numbness? The overthinking that won't shut up? Yeah, no one warns you about that part. But I will.

Here's something else I would like you to know:

This is not your forever.

This isn't where your story ends.

This is where you get to rewrite it, on your terms.

Maybe you've turned into a human lie detector, side-eyeing every promise and overanalyzing every text. Sweet words? Suspicious. Compliments? What's their angle? You used to trust freely. Now? You need a notarized contract just to believe someone means what they say.

Or maybe you are pulling away, not just from the one who betrayed you, but from everyone. Social events?

Exhausting. Letting new people in? Risky. Even your closest friends feel miles away, and you can't decide if you are protecting yourself or just punishing yourself for ever trusting in the first place. And intimacy? Forget it. Letting someone close again feels like handing over the very knife that stabbed you the last time.

Then there's the rage. Oh, the rage. One minute, you are fine. The next? You are fantasizing about flipping tables like a reality TV meltdown. And let's be honest: it's not just them you are mad at. You are mad at yourself, too–for not seeing it coming, for letting your guard down, for caring in the first place.

Some days, though, you are not angry at all. The moment you realize it's almost refreshing, but then you get it.

This is still you.

... Just numb.

You go through the motions, smile when expected, nod in conversations, but you are watching life from behind a glass wall. It's happening, but you are not really in it.

..and please don't even get me started on the overthinking. The mental reruns, the "what-ifs," the endless replay of every moment leading up to the betrayal. What did you miss? What could you have done differently? Spoiler alert: nothing. But try telling your brain that when it's spinning like a hamster on an espresso binge.

Physically? You've been running on fumes. Your body is screaming at you. Maybe it's the tension in your shoulders, the headaches that won't quit, or the stomach that suddenly hates food. Nothing tastes the same, but you keep stress eating anything anyway. And sleep? That's a joke. You are either wide awake at 3 AM, solving crimes that haven't even happened yet, or stuck in nightmares where betrayal plays on loop.

Then there's the worst part, the fear... The fear that this is just who you are now. That the bright, trusting, open version of you is gone. That love is for suckers, and you will never feel safe again.

Maybe you tell yourself that you don't care.

...that you are fine on your own.

But deep down?

You are wondering if you will ever feel whole again.

So, how much of this feels familiar? How much of it has settled into your daily life? If you are nodding along like, *Damn, this is me,* take a step back and ask yourself:

Is this really the future you are signing up for?

Because here's the truth: it doesn't have to be.

You don't need another sign, another red flag, another sleepless night wondering what to do. You've lived out of habit and forgot you can choose.

Time to stop waiting for the universe to take a chance. Stay and rebuild, or walk away and start fresh. Either way, own it. Choose yourself, fully, without apology. Because staying stuck? That's a choice too.

Betrayal doesn't get the final word, you do.

Yeah, it hit hard, but you are not stuck in the fallout. You are absorbing the shock, recalibrating, and stepping into a version of yourself that's sharper, stronger, and absolutely unstoppable.

12- Stop the Ride, Wanna Get Off!!

Don't tell me... you are one of those who stormed out, slammed the door, and thought:

"This is it, I'm done!"

...only to find yourself flipping right into a second round of the same old fart. Or another lover still the same old game. How many 'trial-and-error' hookups are you rocking under that belt? Impressive!

I can just picture you: left hand waving 'goodbye' like you are over it, while the right one's already pulling in the next contender. It's a skill!

...it's freakin' hard to be alone in this world!

Matt's been caught in that emotional whirlwind for years, moving from one girlfriend to the next, always chasing the initial thrill. Deep down, he knows none of them really last. He keeps stepping back into the same empty patterns, not because they make him happy, but because that momentary spark distracts him from the deeper void... but it's a void that never gets filled.

Here is a short movie script of your life: Lately, people love to drop words like validation and, even, conformity, like they are horrible things. Take a minute to consider: we are not individuals. We are social creatures through and through.

Sure, we've got one body to our name, but that body image? That sense of self? Completely built by the world around us, with a hint of personal touch. From the moment we begin to kick around in the womb, we have been tagged with a label: First Name, Last Name, welcome to the game...

Then? We pick up the dreams our parents have laid out for us, like it's part of the damn family inheritance. They drop hints, sometimes in the sweetest ways. Even random strangers throw their two cents in! ...whether they know it or not, those are messages that stuck with us ever since. We work so hard trying to catch a meaningful glimpse of gaze from someone!

Next thing you know, we are following the steps that have been pre-outlined for us. Like a good little soldier, we become the doctor, the lawyer, the perfect husband, or the "ideal" wife. Going into diets or exercising till we drop, just to be fit to fit in. And as easy as that, you are ticking boxes. Dutiful child turned adult, checking off life's list like a champ.

Coming out? Coming out is, in fact, that pivotal moment when you decide to stop failing yourself to avoid failing others. That bold step where you finally put yourself first. Stop living for other people's expectations, and start owning your life, even when you have no freakn' idea of what that means. Nothing feels more powerful and frightening at the same time. Nothing more grown-up or real than that moment.

Let me remind you. As Matt, you have been clinging to the relationship not because it feels good, but because it's better than the emptiness you sometimes feel. Even if you are holding on to your first marriage for dear life, this applies. It's time to break free from this never-ending loop of temporary highs and devastating crashes. You can snatch back the script and write your own damn story.

I know you have shown us all that you can swap that blown-out tire for a donut, and keep on rolling. Now, how far can you really go before it falls apart?

I get it, coming out is scary-like. Like, really scary.

But life's waiting, sexy and bold, on the other side of that rainbow.

Now, picture Matt stepping off that ride. It's not easy, but it's gotta happen. What do you think his life looks like afterward?

Now, here comes Morpheus, offering you the same freakin' choice he gave Neo in *The Matrix*: Do you take the red pill and keep falling back into that fantasy? Yeah, the one you keep patching up every time it falls apart.

...Or grab the blue pill, the one that takes guts but leads to a life where you stand steady, strong, and unapologetically you?

In fact, Neo discovered his superpowers that way.

And guess what? So will you.

Your superpowers aren't flashy laser beams or mind tricks. They are grit, clarity, and the guts to stop putting yourself last. They show up the second you stop performing for everyone else and start living like your own damn hero.

The best things in life take some serious courage, and even more steady work. You have to cross that threshold first, though. It's a rite of passage. Sure, it's gonna sting a little. Hell, maybe a lot. But it won't kill you.

Step out of the revolving door you are stuck in, and grow from betrayal. The bonus? You come out of it stronger, wiser, and not needing anyone to make you feel whole. How hot is that?

Because the real limit? It's the one you create for yourself.

Your superpower, your real flex, is smashing through those self-imposed barriers and fears. Start putting yourself first, and suddenly, the whole damn game changes. No need to wait for anything. Just try it, and see.

Yeah, of course, your therapist might have already thrown around terms like PTSD or even cPTSD, but betrayal? It's a whole different beast. We don't have an official DSM label for betrayal. Yet, here's the key difference that I mentioned before, it's not your body under attack. It's your sense of self. Your freakin' identity. Your agency.

That's what's on the line here.

You are not just patching up a broken heart after confronting mortality. You are defining the very foundation of who you are.

You are becoming loyal... to yourself first, to your truth, to the life you are ready to claim. This is your vow:

Never to shrink.

Never betray yourself again.

Finding that inner gravity, your own personal compass? That's the real deal. It's about being with others, enjoying their company, and negotiating middle ground, all while staying anchored in something unshakable: your inner core.

That self-loyalty is your center of gravity. Your compass. The force that lets you move through the world without losing yourself in it.

Once you've got it, nothing and no one can ever shake you again. It's the best freakin' vaccine against future betrayals.

13- Halfway No More

Yet... here you are, stuck halfway. Not fully in, not totally out. Spinning on the betrayal-reconciliation wheel like a hamster on overdrive. Because, let's be real, this cycle creates a twisted dependency that's freakn' hard to break.

When your sense of self is broken, clinging to someone else can feel like stability.. even when it's just dependence in disguise.

Call it whatever you want, but that's why so many people stay trapped in these toxic spirals, trying to hold onto a sense of integrity, all the while confusing it for love.

It's like being on a runaway train, with every twist and turn unpredictably jolting your heart and mind. You are neither fully in nor completely out, just stuck in limbo, leaving you emotionally drained.

Oh, every beginning is a rush. Every touch feels electric, every smile dripping with hope. A fragile dance where emotions gain speed. Hope pulling you in, hesitation holding you back. Bittersweet, because lurking behind all that heat is suspicion, ready to crash the party. *Is this real this time? How long until it falls apart again?*

As you scan for signs of new betrayals, you want to believe what you hear and see, but every word is tinged with a wave of doubt. Those nagging questions hang in the air, twisting your joy with the constant fear of another letdown.

Then, if betrayal strikes again, the pain is beyond brutal as you are hurled back to square one. The same square one you rushed off, and swore you'd never return to.

Fresh betrayal after trying so hard to rebuild? It stings even worse than the first time. It's not the heartache. It's the anger, the weariness of having let your guard down. Of repeating the cycle, having to start all over. Alone, again.

The thought of piecing together shattered trust, only to face the same crushing end, leaves you drained, desolated, questioning your own sanity, intelligence, and judgment. This cycle of betrayal doesn't break hearts. It crushes spirits.

Take Carla, for instance. Her husband was a pilot, which meant distance was a constant third wheel in their relationship. At first, she thought it was perfect. A way of being together without feeling scrambled. She enjoyed the independence.

As the years went on, the time apart started to wear on her. It felt like living two separate lives: one when he was home, and another when he was gone for days or even weeks. That stretch-and-go rhythm slowly turned into a widening emotional gap, making it harder to reconnect when he was at home.

Sometimes, being together felt incredible. Like the kind of passion straight out of an erotic novel. Other times, it felt as if she was giving room and board to a familiar stranger.

Then Carla found out her husband was cheating. Those wild, fireworks-filled nights? They were the worst days. His way of trying to patch up what he knew was breaking apart. After that, everything unraveled in messy carousel. Waves of forgiveness and moments of closeness, followed by sharp spikes of hate and anger.

So, you decide: in or out, but not in the freakin' middle.

Staying indecisive traps you in an endless loop of emotional turmoil, where each high is shadowed by the fear of falling.

It's draining.

It's disorienting, and it robs you of peace.

Overthinking won't lead you anywhere.

Staying stuck in the middle is not keeping you safe, it's just stretching out the suffering.

Quiet down for a second and pay attention.

Can you hear it?

There's a voice inside that's not screaming.

Not spiraling.

Just whispering.

That's the healthy part of you.

The grounded self.

The one that remembers who you are when everything else feels lost.

Trust it.

Believe in yourself, not blindly, but bravely. Walk forward, and with every step, the path will take shape beneath you. Clarity will come as you step out of the fog and into your power.

14- Make Your Move

Do you know what is the opposite of love? Nope, it is not hate. Hate is a wounded form of love. In fact, psychoanalysts believe that hate is our first emotion when coming into this world[22], as it hurts so much. Love is what happens right after, when we find holding comfort for the very first time.

That's why it is common for divorcees to quarrel for years. They are caught in a cycle of hurt love, unable to let go of the relationship and free themselves for a better next chapter in their lives.

The opposite of love? Neglect[23]. Not the 'go rot in hell' kind of neglect, more of the kind where you let go. Truly let go and let your partner rebuild their life.

...while you rebuild yours.

Why, you ask? Easy. So they can take off and become someone else's problem! Let them glide straight into another inbox while you sit back, sipping your freedom.

---

[22] Carmen González Táboas, personal communication, 2024.

[23] Love is the driving force that leads us to form attachments, and neglect is the absence of that drive when that motivating force is missing or turned off. Then, it feels indifferent either way.

So, what now? You have a choice to make. Here are some basic options:

You can hold onto the relationship and decide to rebuild it brick by brick, giving it the TLC it's been missing. It won't be easy, but maybe if you both roll up your sleeves and dig deep, there's a shot at turning things around.

If you are good at not holding onto grudges...

No, not just biting your tongue–I mean actually letting them go–then the process might even be worth it. You rebuild together, stronger than before, knowing exactly what you are fighting for.

Now, if you are wondering how to kickstart that rebuild... Reverse psychology, my husband might say. As a psychoanalyst, I would rather call in my old friend, Freud: 'Desire is the desire of the other.' We crave what others have.

Do two things: become the one out of reach and make them feel like they are the ones about to lose. Suddenly, the dynamic shifts. That's desire's game, like a dance where stepping back pulls them in.

...Oh, and when they complain? Agree. Smile. Because honestly, you don't give an ash. You are too busy being fabulous, and the universe has your back.

But if the spark's already flickering out, and no amount of stepping back reels them in, you can fold onto the pain, cut your losses, and leave. Sometimes the healthiest thing you can do is walk away, dust off the debris, and reclaim your own life.

If hate is the first emotion we ever feel when we come into this world. Is it also the first thing you feel toward your betrayer? Okay, but here's the deal: this time, own your life.

Owning your life means letting go and learning to stand by your side.

This is not giving up, it's accepting that the relationship is done and dusted. Time to wipe the board clean and give yourself a fresh start. You deserve peace... No shame in that!

Cutting ties feels too final? Not quite ready to make that call? Then take a breather. Pause. Give yourself some time to figure out what you *really* want.

Reevaluate.

You don't need to make a life-altering decision overnight, and there are plenty of options. Let the dust settle, gain some clarity, and see how things unfold before you pick your next move.

It's okay to give yourself space to breathe. Just don't confuse this with settling or slipping back into that old routine of falling for small acts of kindness, forgiving, forgetting and training yourself not to see. No! This space is yours, not for playing the same game all over again.

Of course! So true... the decision might not even be yours to make. It takes two to tango, right? You can't hold something together when the other person's already checked out. It's a two-way street, and if they've mentally packed their bags, what are you really holding on to?

Breathe in your freedom!

Feels good, doesn't it?

...and hey, if you are stuck in the middle because of the kids, why not split the difference? Get a duplex, share the responsibility, and save yourselves from living in the same pressure cooker.

Face this head-on: Whether they stay or go, you still have the power to choose what you want, and move forward on *your* terms. You are not stuck. Their decision doesn't dictate your future, you do.

Whatever you decide, make sure it is rooted in self-loyalty. Not fear. Not guilt. Not habit.

At times you'll feel better than others. You might even convince yourself you are over it. Riding high, feeling strong, thinking, 'I've moved on.'

...Until, bam!

A scent, a song, or a careless comment drags you back, unearthing emotions you thought were long buried.

It may feel like you've regressed to the painful start, but it's not. Each time, you are one step closer to reclaiming your power, your mind, your damn life. One day, this won't be a wound. It'll be a story you outgrew.

By the way, betrayal has a knack for scattering breadcrumbs, teasing your progress and daring you to doubt it. Healing is never a straight line. There's no failure in facing those triggers. They will pass.

You may hesitate.

Yet, do not forget: you are stronger than you think.

Keep going.

As we said, whether due to circumstances, or as a personality trait, we often cling to the familiar, no matter how broken it is. Some people would rather try again than face the fear of flying solo. It's not weakness; it's just human nature.

I listed a few options.

Simply remember: this is *your* choice.

Whether you rebuild, let go, get that duplex, or take a breather, make sure you are doing it for you, not because you are afraid of standing on your own or to avoid hurting anyone.

If you are afraid, know that's totally understandable. You are standing at the bridge of change, and that's a scary place to be.

Yet, know this, change is part of nature.

That's why there are seasons. Forests burn, and what's left is fertile ground. Even when it's raining, the sun is still out, we just can't see it.

Yes, it's scary, but fear fades the moment you take that first step. With each step forward, it softens until one day, it's just a shadow behind you. Things always seem bigger and scarier when you stand still, looking forward at them from the distance.

Your kids? Oh, they might grumble, toss out their opinions, and roll their eyes like it's an Olympic sport. Yet deep down? They want you happy. They might not realize it, or maybe they can't say it out loud, in any case believe me: they know. Your happiness is *their* happiness. Your well-being shapes theirs, even if they don't quite have the words for it yet.

So, for once, put yourself first. I know you might be a little out of practice when it comes to doing that, but you still have it in you. It's like riding a bike. The moment you start focusing on yourself, that old spark will come rushing back ...and honestly? It's long overdue.

Oh, no doubt about it, separation can throw your whole life into a pandemonium, crank up the entropy, and take a swing at your finances and quality of life. But guess what? That chaos is temporary.

Chaos isn't the absence of order. It's the face of transformation, reorganization in motion as everything shifts into new alignment. It's the visible sign that something better is taking shape. That storm? Is not your life falling apart, it's your future falling into place.

I've seen people not just survive, but absolutely thrive once they go their own way. The post-split glow-up? Oh, it's very real.

The fear that's kept you still and stale is not fear of failure, it's fear of failing others. But all this time, you've been failing yourself.

Listen up: the people you are afraid of disappointing? They aren't living your life.

You are.

15- The No BS Real Deal Checklist

For a long time, relationships were about rigid roles, clear-cut expectations of who did what, who led, who followed. Think June Cleaver, dinner on the table at six, and a stiff martini ready for Ward when he walked through the door. Cute, maybe. But let's be real, that's a relic of the past. We don't live in that world anymore, and honestly, why would we want to?

The real challenge today isn't just breaking free from old dynamics–it's figuring out how to build relationships that don't just survive, but actually thrive. And that's where binary relationship theory comes in. It cranks things up a notch. Forget the tired old idea of just "you and me." It's time to think bigger, to recognize the third force at play: you, me, and the relationship itself. A living, breathing force that pulses between us, transforming everything it touches.

That's the difference between a real, hot-blooded partnership and just two people going through the motions. A strong relationship isn't about following a script–it's about mutual respect that doesn't crack under pressure, open communication with no filters, and fiery chemistry that goes deeper than the surface. You are equals, owning your part, with shared goals and no drama hanging over for eternity. It's love, without the BS, when there is...

Mutual Respect: A real relationship that holds steady under pressure. Even when you are at odds, there's a baseline of respect. No cheap shots, no belittling, no "rules for you but not for me," which is a classic sign of control. Just two people who recognize each other's worth, even in the heat of conflict.

Open Communication: And when it comes to communication, there's no second-guessing. You both say what needs to be said. Feelings, thoughts, concerns, all out in the open with zero fear of judgment or payback. You listen, you respond, and even if you don't always agree, at least you are on the same page.

Willingness to Change: But respect and communication mean nothing without willingness to change. Change is not aimed for the usual suspect! Here both of you step up, owning what's going on, and putting in the work to make it right.

Why?

Because at the core, you share the same goals and values. No matter the highs and lows, the connection holds. One of you might be more practical, the other more emotional, but you complement each other, balancing strengths instead of clashing over differences. It's not about sameness, it's about balance and a shared direction. Through it all? You see the future as together. A choice, not pure coincidence.

Intimacy: As I said above, that real connection isn't just something that happens. It is something you both choose to nurture, over and over again. The chemistry? It's fiery, but it runs deeper than physical touch. Built on trust and vulnerability, it's that rare space where you feel completely seen, understood, and safe. And when things go off-track? You don't let distance creep in. You choose to close the gap, to dive right back in and reconnect–body, mind, soul, and everything in between.

Effective Conflict Resolution: But connection alone isn't enough if you can't navigate conflict in a way that strengthens the relationship.

It's not about always seeing eye to eye, it's about acknowledging each other's perspectives, respecting the differences, and staying engaged without resentment.

In a strong relationship, disagreements don't pile up into bitterness; they get worked through, understood, and absorbed into the dynamic. Because it's not about winning, it's about understanding.

Disagreements aren't always about right or wrong, they are about realizing that two different truths can exist at once. Like when I found out that in the U.S., the pepper container has more holes than the salt, while in Argentina, it's the opposite. My husband and I both checked our sources–he asked ChatGPT, I called my sister, Lilly–and sure enough, we each got answers that confirmed our own experience.

Turns out, it wasn't my way or his way. It was both. And isn't that what a binary relationship teaches us? That the goal isn't to prove a point, but to recognize that every gesture is an opportunity to take in the bigger picture. That reality isn't always one-size-fits-all.

Accountability: In a binary relationship, accountability is more than owning your mistakes, it's about recognizing how your actions shape the relationship itself. No blame-shifting, no weaponizing past mistakes.

Winning an argument? You know very well that only lasts so long, while hurting the overall relationship in the meantime. Instead, you both show up, taking responsibility for your part in the dynamic, and doing the work to keep the relationship strong.

And here's the key: when one of you is upset, it's seen as a private moment of relief or a reaction to the relationship… not a personal attack. That slight detachment? Game changer. It allows you to step back, get curious, and actually listen without getting defensive. It shifts accountability from guilt and blame to understanding and action. Because when both of you see challenges as something to address together, accountability stops feeling like pressure and starts feeling like a path forward, growth, and an opportunity for mutual connection.

Healthy Independence: At the end of the day, here's no possessiveness, no controlling behavior, no keeping tabs. Instead, both of you maintain a healthy independence, with separate interests and friendships that actually strengthen your bond rather than threaten it. Because real love isn't about ownership, it's about freedom.

Support During Hard Times: Of course, at some point, life throws its curveballs. What then? You don't turn away. You lean in. In a binary relationship, support isn't about one person carrying the full weight. It's about the relationship itself acting as the stabilizer. It holds steady, absorbs the impact, and redistributes the load.

One of you might be struggling, but that doesn't mean the other becomes the sole lifeline. This isn't martyrdom–it's partnership. Maybe one of you steps in with logistics while the other provides emotional grounding. Maybe one takes the lead for a while, knowing the roles will shift again. There's no scorekeeping, no silent resentment, no tallying of who did more.

Wouldn't you say? ...Every challenge is a test. A reality check. Those shifting logistics? They reveal what's truly worth doing and what's just noise.

Hard times aren't just obstacles. They are refreshing opportunities for bold moments, for stepping up, shaking off what no longer serves you, and proving to yourselves what your relationship is really made of.

Neither you nor your partner will check off every box here, and that's okay. The real question is: how are you both doing in the areas that matter most to you? Are you putting in the work where it truly counts, or are you ignoring more red flags than you can handle? Clinging to a few checked boxes so tightly that you are living with one eye shut to reality?

Clearly, you are both responsible for the health of the relationship, not just for your own satisfaction, or to fulfill each other's need for validation. You both contribute to the health of the relationship itself by nurturing that synergy. And why? Because what's good for the system? ...It's even better for you.

16- Fix or Nix: Work on It or Slam the Door

Another chapter on going in circles? Yawn. Boring!! Let me tell you something–this is just a book. Now, imagine if it were your life. You gonna keep spinning, or are you ready to break free?

Because, let's be real... you've already decided to patch things up with your ex, right? ...Or maybe you've swiped right on their doppelgänger.... same package, just fresh wrapping. Is that love? Or muscle memory.

Either way, you are facing the same question: fix what's broken or walk away for good? Staying stuck in the middle isn't just uncomfortable: it's exhausting.

Unless you are ready to confront not just the sting of betrayal but the deeper scars you have been dragging around since childhood, you are on a fast track to same mess, different day.

Yes, we're wired deep from childhood, which sets us up for what's called repetition compulsion. And no, this isn't about blaming your parents, it's just how we're built.

Repetition compulsion is a fancy way of saying we're drawn to familiar dysfunction, like moths to a flame. Add to that your fresh burns from betrayal, and you've got the perfect recipe for things to go off the rails.

When betrayal smacks us in the face, we don't just feel the sting: we armor up. If we weren't already wired to be needy or evasive straight out of life's oven, betrayal cranks up the heat. Suddenly, we're either clinging for dear life, desperate for constant reassurance (anxious), or slamming emotional doors shut, locking people out before they get too close (avoidant).[24]

It hits even harder when things start to feel real, when love is on the line and the stakes are sky-high.

Unless you shake things up and actually face what's lurking under the surface, you'll keep spinning the same old wheel. ...and you know how that story ends. Time to break the pattern before the pattern breaks you.

The 3AM Wake-Up Call

I still remember those first few months after marrying Harry. He had built us this stunning house, our

---

[24] Given the right circumstances, anyone can hide away. Yet, those with more dependent traits often stay emotionally attuned to their significant others. In contrast, avoidant types tend to pull away more completely, appearing numb or distant.

dream home where we still live. Yet mornings were a quiet battlefield for me. Every day, I had to dig through my suitcase to piece together something to wear for work, piling up frustration one outfit at a time. I wanted to say something, but I couldn't figure out how. My English back then wasn't great, and I felt stuck in silence.

Then it happened. One night, out of nowhere, I woke up at 3AM and said it ...in full-blown Spanish. Harry calls this my uh-uh moment because, as he tells it, he jolted awake to the sound of me blurting out something he couldn't make heads or tails of. Just me, mid-rant, probably waving my hands in the dark. Classic.

So, once you get to meet someone, moving in with your partner often feels like the logical next step. It saves money, and hey, it's romantic, right?

But once the boxes are unpacked -or not- you start noticing things you hadn't before. The garlic-scented air, the too-small closet, their habit of skipping showers, you name it,...

You brush it off, convincing yourself it does not worth the fight. You fold, you give in. Until a minor disagreement spirals into a full-blown argument.

...or you wake up at 3AM, like I did.

Then it hits you, like a cold splash of water. You don't even have a drawer to call your own. Your furniture is in storage. You moved into someone else's territory, and it feels more visiting than fully living in it.

What's worst, your old apartment keys? Gone.

Your situation turned unstable. You? Stuck.

Panic sets in, topped off with a heavy splash of... *What the hell do I do now?*

Never move into someone else's place without setting up equal conditions.

It's not just about space for your stuff. The furniture discussion? That is not the issue. That is the excuse to quarrel over something way deeper, your shrinking sense of agency since the moment you moved in.

I get it, you are still caught up in the connection, still holding onto that fire, even if it's flickering under the weight of daily life. You've wanted to bring this up from the start, but you keep swallowing the words. It's awkward. You don't want to make waves. You don't want to hurt their feelings or, worse, make the magic fade even faster.

But listen, avoiding this? That's what's going to hurt you the most. And when you are hurting, I assure you, it won't just be you who feels it.

Always, start the hard talks before you unpack your bags, because when you realize you are in an uneven relationship, your world, your options, will start to feel small and cramped, skyrocketing your anxiety.

Sarah's Slow Disappearance

For the better part of five years, Sarah and Kurt had been stuck in an on-again/off-again, rinse, repeat. Sure, when it was good, it was electric. But every time they got close, something cracked. Fights erupted over stupid things... unwashed dishes, ignored texts, the dog's bad habits. But Sarah knew, deep down, it was never really about the dishes.

When they sat across from me, they hit me with the classic line every couple brings in: "We have a problem of communication."

Here's the thing, every relationship has its highs and lows. That's normal. But when the lows start stacking up, when tension becomes the default setting, that's your signal to pause and ask: What's actually happening here?

Because what you might call "communication issues" is often the surface of a deeper gap. You might even believe you know exactly what is happening, but getting it through to the other side has been incredibly frustrating. So, you ended up calling it "issues with communication."

Can these problems be worked through with some real effort and commitment? Or is the emotional turbulence too much to handle? Are you hanging on for a possible real joy, or dragging out the inevitable heartbreak?

Sometimes, the relationship is over before we are even ready to admit it.

Sometimes, we need to work on ourselves before working on the relationship.

For Sarah, it wasn't just the fights. It was the nagging question that wouldn't leave her alone: Where do I actually stand in Kurt's life?

At first, being with him felt like stepping into the spotlight. His friends admired her, and yeah, she didn't exactly hate the attention. Even when something about it felt a little off, almost staged, there was still that rush, that little high of feeling desired.

But once the novelty wore off, something shifted. She started feeling less like a person and more like a prop. And then it hit her, those moments when Kurt paraded her around? They were never really about her. It was about him. It was Kurt showing off, looking like the guy who had it all while she stood beside him like a trophy.

Sarah used to be lively and social, the kind of person who thrived in a crowd. After being with Kurt for a while, she realized something had shifted. She no longer had a personal life. She had become someone she barely recognized.

Looking back, it all clicked: Kurt had been chipping away at her world, piece by piece. His comments were never outright cruel, just subtle enough to stick.

A little dig about her friends here, a sigh of disapproval when she got home late there. At first, it seemed harmless. Just relationship stuff. But little by little, she started pulling back. Don't get me wrong. It was never her decision. Nope! This seeps in more subtly.

Not because he forced her to...

Not because she was bending to his will.

She just... Stopped!

An insidious shift.

A slow, quiet fading of who she was.

A silent erasure of self.

Because sometimes a whisper, a sigh, a raised eyebrow sinks in even harder. Until one day, you look around and realize you are not you anymore. Just a version of yourself that fits them.

Somewhere along the way, the things that once made Sarah feel alive didn't even cross her mind anymore. Then, the full picture came into focus. She wasn't special–she was convenient. The shiny car. The good job. The VIP tickets to the game. And just like that, another crack ran through her heart.

Was he with her? Or with the perks that came with her?

Once trust starts to shake, the whole foundation feels like it could collapse at any moment. Yet, when she was pulling away, Kurt would swoop in, promising her the moon and stars like he was some kind of fairytale prince. Yeah, at first, she ate it up, who wouldn't?

He always knew what to say, hitting all the right notes, like a script written just for her. Let's face it, it wasn't about the words. It was about not being alone. Because having someone, almost anyone, close feels so much better than the alternative, right?

Soon enough, his promises started to feel hollow. She wanted to believe him, she really did. Of course, after hearing the same sweet talk on repeat, it was like his words lost their magic.

Reality never quite caught up to his big declarations, and the gap between what he promised and what he actually did was impossible to ignore. She wanted to believe him. But facts don't lie. And the facts? They never quite measured up.

The Narcissist's Playbook

Then came the next grand gesture, couples' therapy. Kurt's idea. Sounds promising, right? He even scheduled the first session himself, so thoughtful. And since his wife was so busy, he graciously offered to handle the intake on his own.

Now, if that doesn't set off alarm bells, I don't know what does.

For any therapist, that move is a flashing red flag. When one partner tries to control the story from the start, it's rarely about fixing things. It's about framing them. And that? That's a whole different game.

Let's be real, I just painted you a narcissist. Not the loud, obvious kind, but the charming, reasonable, thoughtful kind. The kind who makes you want to believe. But what's the real goal here? It sure as hell isn't saving the relationship because he values Sarah for her. Oh no.

Narcissists don't see people as separate, whole beings with their own needs, desires, and inner lives. They see them as extensions of themselves, as fuel. Their sense of other is stunted, frozen in an early stage of emotional development. Sarah isn't a partner to him; she's a source. A steady drip of attention, to fill Kurt's endless void.

And therapy? It's not about fixing what's broken, because in his mind, he's not the problem. It's about keeping the game in play. Controlling the narrative. Making sure Sarah stays just tangled enough that she won't leave.

That's why narcissists are so skilled at manipulating the narrative. It's not just deception, it's survival. Whether they paint themselves as the hero, the victim, or the misunderstood genius, the goal is always the same: attention, validation, control. Because without that? They feel like nothing.

She gives him that steady stream of emotional fuel and stability, and there's no way he's giving that up. Even if it means twisting the whole therapy game to keep her locked in.

As I've said before, sometimes it's way easier to stick with the devil you know than to face the one you don't. For Sarah, breaking up was like climbing out of hell itself. She had clipped her wings so much, she couldn't even hear her own inner compass anymore.

Please, understand: I'm not here to hand out roadmaps with a big shiny "finish line, you are out and saved" stamped on them. If I did that, if any other psychotherapist were to do that, Sarah would be swapping one commander for another. First Kurt, now the therapist (me). That's not how we roll. That adds to her being stuck in the same old dependency, waiting for someone else to tell her where to go or what to do.

Many times, with new patients, I explain that therapy is this special space where you finally get to meet yourself. It's not some casual chat. You don't need to bring your pain, you can also bring your joy. In fact, bring whatever you want. For all of it makes to those rich, serendipitous moments in which you discover yourself.

If you run home, all excited to share your insights, the emotional charge falls apart, and poof... the magic fades.

Therapy? Not for broadcasting.

It's where you meet you, and the work you do happens within you.

Sarah kept getting pulled back in by Kurt's sweet promises and those honey-moon phases that eventually made her second-guess everything. Somewhere deep in her bones, she had to know being with someone like

Kurt and these cycles of trust and betrayal were watering down her self-worth.

That's usually how it goes: the quiet truth sits there waiting to be faced. Sarah wasn't ready yet. Even if it meant silencing that aching feeling every time she tried to push it down, she chose to remain comfortably uncomfortable, avoiding the nuance that demanded confrontation.

So, Sarah (and all the Sarahs of the world, after all this is not my patient's real name), if you are reading this, know that delaying the inevitable doesn't fix a damn thing. It keeps you spinning, stuck in that hurtful endless loop ...and as your therapist? I'm not here to be your new commander. I'm here to be your best tool, at your service for you to take charge of your life. You call the shots. My job is to help you find that inner compass again, so that you can follow it.

Because the real power? It's already in you.

This Isn't Just a Choice. It's Your Damn Life

So, choose! Go fix or nix, but end the confusion for you, your partner, and everyone else involved. It takes guts to stand firm in your decision.

Reality check:

You can't have it all.

Staying stuck isn't neutral, it's a choice to stay in pain.

Not ready to decide? That's still a decision by default.

...and guess what? It's the riskiest decision of all. Not only do you keep spinning in that soul-crushing limbo, but you also miss out on every benefit that comes with actually *choosing*.

High stakes, zero payoff.

Pick your path and throw everything you have got into making it successful, exciting, truly worthwhile.

Life is tough, and it demands hard work to be rewarding. Roll up your sleeves, dig in, and push hard. It won't be easy, but the sooner you start, the quicker you will see results and the longer you will reap the rewards.

Examine the patterns I'm laying out before you, and be honest in your responses. Understand the gravity of what's at stake: Your freakin' life. Focus on how serious this is. Nothing else matters as much as getting this right.

Let me rephrase this, getting it right is not about coming with the brilliant solution.

Nope!

It's all in the effort you put in after the decision is made.

Nothing in - Nothing out.

Go all in, and you will see a brilliant outcome.

What do I mean by this? Have you considered that the only person responsible for your happiness, joy, satisfaction, success -whatever you want to call it- is you and mainly you?

Just you.

So when trust turns into complains over demanded expectations, and those unmet expectations morph into betrayal, who's really at fault for that hurt? It's not always so clear, is it?

At the end of the day, it's your expectations and beliefs running much of this show. Shaping how you feel about trust and disappointment, that's the part you have to own.

Becoming responsible for your path to fulfillment and happiness? That is the very first step. You can't get there without claiming it for yourself first. Stop waiting for someone else to deliver it. Grab the wheel and steer yourself toward the life you want, because no one else can do it for you.

I can hear you all the way from here: '*But how do I even start? You are still not telling me how!*' But I have, since the very beginning:

No more autopilot,

Change your attitude,

Learn who you are,

...and put what matters to you first.

Also, don't engage with perfectionism, procrastination, overanalyzing, self-doubt, people-pleasing, or fear of failure—all those excuses keep you stuck. Stuck in the need for validation, living outside in instead of reaching your potential through autonomy. The moment you obsess over it, you are caught in a loop. Let it go. Don't make it a thing. The more you fixate, the stronger its grip. Breathe, act, move forward.

Socrates nailed it: It's not what you have, but how you handle yourself with it. Wealth, health, love, they are only as good as your ability to own them without them owning you. Happiness is a pursuit, you get to enjoy a bit as you move forward in the decisions you make.

Ask yourself: What's distracting me from my path? What habits, commitments, or even relationships do I need to release to reach my potential, my goals, my woo?

That's it.

Stop overcomplicating it.

The moment you start prioritizing what truly matters to you, everything else will begin to fall into place.

Give it time.

Trust the process,

...and avoid betraying yourself.

Every step you take can either bring you closer to or farther from the life you dream of. Each small gesture brings you closer ...or keeps you distant. It's all in how you engage, what you choose. Make it count.

Autonomy

Please remember, autonomy doesn't mean cutting yourself off from others, nor does it mean bulldozing your way through. Rather, it's about moving past the rivalry of two, as we explored in Chapter One, while staying true to yourself.

Autonomy is connecting the dots you've been too busy–or too afraid–to look at. It's seeing the full picture instead of just the pieces you are comfortable with.

Because once those dots connect, once you become fully aware ...there's no more running, no more pushing through, no more stuffing things into hidden corners just to keep the peace. You stop managing life and start living it–with your eyes wide open. No more keeping things afloat that were never meant to last. No more bending yourself to fit where you don't belong.

Autonomy isn't just about making choices... it's about owning them.

From that self-commitment, the natural flow is toward relationships where both people nurture not just each other, but also the relationship itself as a distinct, living entity.

What is a couple? A relationship shouldn't be a cage or a slow shift from something amazing into heavy work, confusion, and constant compromise. Noooo! What if it felt like a supportive breathing space. A place where individuality and connection don't compete, but actually coexist?

In a healthy binary relationship, it's not about winning, controlling the fight, or spinning the narrative. It's not about leading, following, or losing yourself in someone else. It's about creating a space where both of you feel valued, respected, and seen. A space where love isn't a power struggle but a rhythm where giving and receiving happen naturally, without keeping score.

How? By nurturing the relationship itself, not just the other person.

You are free, and you let the other person be their own, true to themselves. You are both autonomous. And with that clarity and awareness? You know who you are, and you know what you bring to the table.

That type of connection takes effort, negotiation, and a willingness to move beyond what works for just one of you to discover what sustains you both. But it's a different sort of effort: one that builds up. Not one where a single person carries the heavy load, watching their dreams fade while keeping everything afloat.

A great place to start? Go solo for a while.

If you've been feeling like I push for divorce, let me tell you something: You can be with whoever you want. It's your life! I'm just your biggest fan, here to tell you that if you truly want to make it work this time, there's only one way: first, you need a period of detox celibacy. Not as punishment, but as a way to clear the noise and reconnect with yourself. Because, if you don't know who you are, how can you contribute to a relationship instead of just clinging to it?

Can you see it? Try a full reset before deciding who's worth your time.

Betrayal knocked you off balance, right?

So now, it's about getting a grip on your thoughts, emotions, and actions. But this time, leveling up. How? By locking in your self-definition.

Self-definition, autonomy, is what keeps you steady, grounded, and moving with purpose. Then you'll know if someone truly aligns with you or if they are just a passing craving. Like ice cream ...sweet, tempting, and gone in minutes. Feels good? Sure. Nourishing? Not a chance.

Detox isn't about avoiding love or locking yourself away. It's a hard reset, wiping out the noise, clearing the emotional debris, and giving yourself the space to finally hear your own voice.

Become an independent soul.

Learn to be loyal to yourself.

Then, go decide.

Be selective... Pick not out of convenience, nostalgia, or hidden motives, but from a place of wholeness. Find someone who complements you, not completes you– because you were never broken to begin with[25].

---

[25] If you see your lack as proof of your imperfection, flip the script. Being human is an incredibly beautiful and perfect creation— precisely because you are imperfect. That space, that longing, that 'missing piece' isn't a flaw; it's what propels you to move, to create, to connect. It's what makes freedom possible.

Since birth, you learned to depend on others for survival, and it worked. It had to. But as an adult, clinging to that same instinct can cost you something far greater–your self-loyalty.

...And the worst part? You don't even see it happening until betrayal hits like a wake-up call.

That's why true connection isn't about finding a team-player to numb the ache of loneliness or soothe an emptiness. It's about choosing a person you respect -maybe even admire a little- to witness your life. It's about standing whole and choosing someone whose presence amplifies, not diminishes, who you are. That's when you start building a relationship as a third element, something you create together, not something that shackles you.

It's totally up to you if you choose to go back to your partner, your Jay Whozit. Just make sure Jay has grown too.

My advice? Don't go back to a bad habit just because it's familiar. You've elevated yourself. Don't shrink back down to fit into an old dynamic that no longer serves you.

Love should expand you. Love contains, it holds you steady while giving you the freedom to fly. If you have to clip your own wings to make it work, that's not love.

That's someone getting comfortable at your expense. You deserve more than that.

Bottom line: Autonomy and self-definition mean nothing if you keep abandoning who you are at the moment someone walks in.

Self-loyalty means that no matter who comes, who goes, or who stays,... you never leave yourself.

Because at the end of the day, it's not just about choosing the right partner. It's about building a relationship that actually honors who you are. Every. Single. Time. And from that unshakable place? That's when you build something real.

Loyalty starts with you. Keep that promise, and everything else will fall into place.

When love feels lonely

Flying solo is not your thing? Living with a narcissist and certain other personality types, can be a way of flying solo, too. It is being on your own while with someone. Narcissists can hardly care about anyone other than themselves, no matter how much space they take up in your life.

If you went from feeling fantastic to feeling like you are sharing your life but carrying all the emotional weight alone, that's a major hint. Don't fool yourself into thinking that leaving them will destroy them -whether it's a him or her, because narcissistic PD doesn't pick a gender.

The moment you walk out that door, they'll start searching for their next fix to feed that endless craving for attention. You are not their lifeline: you are merely part of their supply chain.

Taking someone home for sex? That can feel like you are connecting while really being alone, all at once. It's not true intimacy, is it? In the beginning, it can seem like you are getting what you need without giving too much away. It might sound thrilling, even empowering. But over time, each encounter can start to leave you a little more drained, a little more empty, as if something essential is slipping away. It's less about connection and more about the chase. The sport.

The same thing happens when you hold onto someone just to fill the void. You are not giving it your whole heart, you are leaning on them to patch up an emotional need. That's why separation feels terrifying no matter who you are with. You can be great at switching one person for another, which is your constant attempt at filling the emptiness. It might feel like love, but... Is it? It's an artifice to avoid facing what you need to work on, to manage the anxiety of facing life solo.

The best relationships aren't a crutch or a bandaid for our wounds; they are a partnership that challenges us to be better, grow stronger, and give as much as we receive. That kind of satisfaction is worth the effort ... and it starts with knowing yourself first.

I get it, having someone by your side can feel incredible. Sometimes, it's the thing that makes you feel seen, like you finally have worth, like you indeed matter. But don't just grab onto anyone: be selective. Hold onto your integrity.

Once you have mastered being alone, you'll know who you are and how to stay true to yourself, even when you are with others. You'll stand tall beside the right one, not because you need them, but because you have decided to be with this person.

This is your life. Imagine what real love looks like -feel it, define it- so you have something solid to aim for when the time comes.

Real love is not butterflies in the stomach. That is lovely and feels incredible. But it's not it.

Real love is a two-way street, that starts with self-love.

Master being alone, and you'll find that when you stand fully in your truth, you'll choose someone who stands beside you, not over you or under you. That's where true connection begins. And it's worth every bit of effort.

17- Strategic Choices in Troubled Homes

I know, it's the world's least-fun reality show. All the sudden you are not partners in crime anymore: You are awkward roommates navigating the same sinking ship. A whole lot of sharing space, biting your tongue, and praying you don't kill each other before this chapter ends.

Is this chapter fun to read? Probably not.

The one you need? Absolutely, and don't skip the Quick & Dirty Coexistence toolkit bellow! You need to hear all this, and get yourself ready. Because you cannot sit there undecided and drilled the rest of your life.

Is the betrayal something recent? Let's get one thing straight: your safety comes first. If the betrayal is recent and tensions are high, now is the time to think tactically, not emotionally.

Pick your battlegrounds wisely. Keep your exits clear, your safe zones mapped, and if things heat up, head for the street, not the stove. Loop in a friend, a family member, or even a nosy neighbor. Someone who can step in if you need backup. Have a go-bag ready (yes, like a spy on the run). Clothes, documents, essentials, because scrambling in a crisis? Not the move.

If the cops show up, take names, take badge numbers, and take notes. And don't forget: stay as cool as if you were stretched out on a beach, soaking up the sun. Keep that image, hold that vibe as you take a few breaths in to remain calm, collected, and completely unshaken.

Lastly, before you storm out in frustration, and shut the door behind you for good... know your rights. In some places, leaving the house could cost you more than your peace. It could cost you your claim to it. Stay smart, stay strategic, and never let them see you lose your cool.

Yes, as you said it... you might end up stuck in roommate mode for a while. But don't sit there like a bystander. Take charge and make your space *yours*. You deserve a livable space. Even if you end as awkward roommates, you still have a say. Set the vibe on your terms. Start by checking the Quick & Dirty toolkit in the annex, and carve out your personal spaces.

Oh.. and if you are thinking a cutthroat attorney is going to get you half of everything... Think again. In reality, you'll probably be shelling out big bucks in legal fees, and property rarely gets divided as "fairly" as you would hope. Especially if there's a trust involved, things get murky, fast. You might end up with less than you bargained for.

And if you think you are going to spill it all in a tell-all book, pouring out your suffering for the world to see– think again. Turns out, heartbreak isn't just yours to share. Half of that story? It belongs to your partner. And if you are not careful, you might end up paying copyright fees for a trauma that wasn't solely yours to publish.

When life feels like it's falling apart, it's hard to focus, let alone handle all the details. When you want to save money while still getting great legal advice, think about using a mediator, or use your lawyer more as an advisor. You handle the basic stuff -phone calls, emails, gathering paperwork- and let your lawyer guide you on how to do all you need to get done. It's more affordable, the job still gets done, and you can trust that every "t" is crossed and every "i" is dotted.

Let's be blunt: a shoulder to cry on is great, but it won't pay the bills. Build a pro-team that keeps you rolling. Besides an attorney, you'll probably need a financial advisor. Most people think financial advisors are only for the wealthy, but the right one? A total game-changer.

They'll help you track assets—including the ones your partner "forgot" to mention—so your attorney knows exactly what to go after. They'll map out what life actually looks like post-divorce—what you can afford, what's worth fighting for, and how to make sure you don't wake up one day wondering where it all went.

Pro tip: Skip the big firms that treat you like a case file. Find an advisor who listens, strategizes with you, and sends you into that attorney's office knowing exactly what you need—not just what you think you deserve. Because let's be real: financial clarity isn't just power—it's survival.

So, have you decided to stop spinning? Great! Then, its time to tell you, there are two ways to go about this: nice or dirty.

Going dirty? It's expensive on every level, and money is the least of it. Your blood pressure will spike, your mood will tank, and your sanity? Let's just say, lawyers aren't the only ones who'll be cashing in.

You'll be exhausted, constantly replaying every argument, every petty move. Stress will eat you alive, and your body will remind you...tight chest, clenched jaw, sleepless nights. And legally? The longer and nastier this gets, the more you lose.

Judges don't reward the loudest person, they reward the most put-together one. If you show up swinging, you might just swing yourself right out of credibility.

What's the real goal? Is winning so important? Is it worth dragging yourself (and maybe even your kids) through all of this? ...or would you rather be free and have a life to enjoy?

Right now, you might be feeling lost and fired up, but revenge is a boomerang. It always comes back around. Do you really want to be carrying this same fire twenty years from now?

Close your eyes and picture it: You are at your kid's graduation, their wedding, or maybe holding your first grandchild. Will you look back and be proud of how you handled this divorce? Or will you wish you have done it differently?

So, what's it going to be, going dirty or keeping it clean?

Because going dirty doesn't just drain your wallet.

It drains your life.

You can also go clean... You both negotiate how to end this story like actual adults. Letting go of each other while recognizing that, for now, you still share a roof and, more importantly, the kids. This way, you keep the headaches in check, avoid turning your home into a battlefield, and, let's be real, make life easier for everyone in the long run.

The moment you decide to fold your cards and move on, here's the best advice you'll get: channel every ounce of that anger into building the next chapter of your life, not into fighting your ex. The more you throw punches, the worse, longer and more expensive it will be for you.

18- Stepping Up Without Stepping Over

If you don't have children, awesome, I'll see you in the next chapter.

If you do, this chapter is short and to the point. For all the practical how-tos, check out the Co-Parenting Playbook in the annex.

First, let's get one thing straight: Family isn't a house, a last name, or even a living arrangement. It's a network of relationships. What truly matters is the connection, consistency, and presence you bring to your child's life.

No one–and I mean no one–can give your child what you do when you are fully present with them. It's in those little moments: the way you light up when they smile, cheer them on at their games, or sneak off for a lunch date. That's how they learn their worth.

Being a parent isn't easy on the best days. But when you are in the thick of your own pain. When all you want is to shut the world out and steal five minutes to just breathe, it can feel downright impossible. You are heartbroken and running on fumes. And yet, these kids need you. They need you sober and strong, not as someone to lean on but as the solid ground beneath their feet.

Here's the twist: this demand for strength, even when you feel like you have nothing left in your tank, might just be what keeps you from falling apart entirely. Showing up for them, even in your most vulnerable moments, is an anchor—a way to stay steady while you find your footing again.

For those of us who tend to withdraw when life gets tough, stepping back might feel like the easiest option. But distance can quickly become a wall. Once that wall is up, shame keeps the distance alive, whispering that you are failing them, that you are not enough—and that only creates more distance. Your kids don't need perfection. They need presence. Let them remind you why staying connected matters. Even when it's hard, showing up is the first step to healing—for both of you.

And for those of us who hover—micromanaging every decision, sending endless texts, or struggling to give them breathing room—pause for a moment. Overprotection can stifle their confidence and independence. Sometimes the most loving thing you can do is step back and trust them to find their own way. It's not about letting go entirely; it's about offering enough space for them to build resilience, knowing you are there when it counts.

I had dinner with a university dean a couple of weeks ago. She told me she's overwhelmed by parents who overstep, especially the ones showing up to Job Fair day. Let me tell you, it's not a good look to walk into a job interview with Mom or Dad in tow. If you want your kid to succeed, release! And right now–when you are already going through a life-changing phase yourself–is the perfect time to start.

So, this is the moment when you and the other parent get to decide: nice or dirty in regards to parenting.

Go nice, and you have a real shot at seeing your kids happy. Go dirty? Get ready for constant heartbreaks and bills, legal fees, therapy costs, and stress that never quits.

..and it doesn't stop there. Every holiday, graduation, and milestone ahead? Now a logistical nightmare. Your kids will be stuck juggling seating charts, crossing their fingers that things don't explode, or worse: they'll just stop inviting you altogether.

Honestly, nothing says 'I love you' like not making them pick sides every holiday table for the next twenty years.

Decided on nice? Smart move!

From now on, you are a team when it comes to raising these kiddos. How do you build a good team? By respecting each other.

Yup, even when you don't agree.

So, save the eye-rolls and huffing about their slip-ups for private conversations. Especially not in front of the kids! If your child brings it up, just listen and keep your response neutral.

Ah, and since we're at it... let's drop the whole "grieving process" narrative.

Has someone died? No. Your kids still have both parents, just new arrangements. They don't need to grieve; they need to adapt.

Stop making your grief theirs.

Your kids don't need saving. You do.

Unmesh! Be free!

If you want your kids to ace your divorce, show them you've got it handled.

Your main focus? Keeping things steady for the kids without losing yourself in the process.

Your kids want to stay with your betrayer? The same answer applies to any experience as long as it's safe: Support their exploratory efforts and let them discover life for themselves.

And since we're at it... Are you one of those who feels the need to do the exact opposite of what your parents did? Preaching boundaries, yet struggling to set clear limits with your own kid? What a contradiction, right?

Too much or too little, both are extremes.

Think of limits and rules not as restrictions, but as tools. Like a screwdriver, they help anchor the floor beneath your child. Too hard? It's rigid and harsh on the knees. Too soft? It turns to mud, or worse, quicksand. Without that solid ground, kids can't find clarity or feel their worth reflected in their parents' eyes.

Afraid of becoming your parent? Worried your kid might reject you if you set limits? That fear is common. And ironically, the rejection you are so anxious about is often your child acting out their fear of not being worthy. As I told you before, that's not defiance. It's pain.

So go ahead, create a new kind of parenting. One built on clear, consistent lines that mark what's safe and stable, especially after the shake-up of separation or divorce.

For more on this, see the Co-Parenting Playbook. In the meantime, remember: the more you forbid something, the more desirable it becomes.

Doubts along the way? Picture your kid in therapy at 30, spilling about their life. What do you want them to say?

Really. The moment you release, let go, and start prioritizing what actually deserves your time and energy, you are not being selfish–you are getting stronger. You stop following someone else's map and start leading with your own compass. Your happiness isn't a luxury; it benefits everyone.

There's a big difference between strength and selfishness. Egotism is bulldozing through life without a care for anyone else. Generosity is not passing on leftovers. It is giving with purpose, sharing in a way that actually matters. So be generous, starting with yourself. Get stronger, not just for you, but for your ability to love and lead with intention.

19- Is There a Healthy One Left Standing?

Wondering how to spot a healthy one? Tricky question, right? The basic answer? Start by asking yourself: *is this person a good listener?*

I mean, not just someone who smiles and nods to make you feel great while you talk. No, that's sweet, yeah.. that's not it.

I'm talking about the kind of listening that shows they *get you*. Like, if you mention you don't like dark chocolate, do they remember and get you milk chocolate next time? Or do they keep bringing you the dark stuff because they think they know better?

That's the difference right there.

You've probably been told to watch out for narcissists. But have you heard of waxies or Machiavellians? It's time to bring some fresh air to this conversation.

Narcissists might be the poster children of toxic relationships, but they're not the only ones who can twist your world into a mess. Plus, they do have an awesome side that works well for some people.

But take the waxies, for instance. As described by Bion, they "attack the link" between emotional and mental processes. The result? They are masters of the cold shoulder. Don't mistake their detachment for assertiveness, it's not. They might seem cool, but they are closed off, unreachable, like nothing can touch them. It's emotional sabotage, pure and simple. A shield to avoid connection.

...and the Machiavellians? Oh, they're the grandmasters of manipulation. Strategic, ruthless, and always three steps ahead. Think of them as chess players on steroids, moving people like pawns to serve their agenda. Unlike psychopaths, they're not impulsive; every move is calculated.

While they can read emotions, it's not to connect. It's to control. Cold empathy, weaponized. That's what sets them apart from narcissists, who are too busy soaking up admiration to play the long game. In fact, next to a Machiavellian's icy precision, some narcissists almost look... harmless.

Almost.

All of them might charm you, make you laugh, or even ignite something that feels genuine. But don't be fooled. Their toxic tendencies can twist your world into a full-blown mess before you know it.

Be smart. Admit it. It is not always about dodging a specific "bad" personality type. Years ago, borderline personality disorder had a bad reputation.

Wouldn't you say it is not the person, but the dynamic and how we handle ourselves that makes or breaks things?

Meaning? Meaning how you engage.

A Machiavellian can only play chess if we keep stepping onto their board.

A narcissist can only thrive on admiration if we keep feeding it.

Just remember what you bring to the relationship

...not only what you get out of it.

Binary Relationship Theory

A healthy relationship has three essential elements: you, me, and the relationship itself. Remember? When it's just two, rivalry creeps in.

Thanks to our ability to stay lost in fantasy, it always starts the same way:

Me + You = To the moon.

But too often, it shifts...

Me vs. You = A slow-burning war.

The relationship is that shared space where we both bring something uniquely ours. When we respect that space, we create something neither of us could build alone. Like a triangle, it stays strong when all three sides are valued and nurtured.

First off, like I've said before, you need to be your own person. No losing yourself in them, no sacrificing your life just to keep the relationship alive. You both keep your sense of self while growing together, creating something bigger than any of you alone.

Being with someone should feel like a joyful adventure -never like walking on eggshells. It's about waking up and thinking, 'I'm lucky to have this person by my side.'

You want their support and guidance, but you should also feel free to make your own choices. A healthy partnership embraces differences without taking them personally or doubting the care between you. That's the secret sauce: respect, support, and the freedom to be yourself.

Oh! ...and here's an incredible ingredient: admiration. Admiring the person you are with lifts both of you up. But -big warning- it should never come at the cost of overshadowing your own strengths and successes. It's not about one dimming their lights so that the other one shines brighter.

Hear me out, I didn't say idealization. Admiration and idealization are very different.

Idealization puts someone on a pedestal, wrapping them in our expectations and desires until they seem larger than life. It might feel magnificent for a while, but it's not real. It's an emotional illusion that blinds us to their true self. And in that blinding, we start to feel small. Like we can't measure up, like we need them to feel whole. But that's only because we've unknowingly projected our best traits onto them.

We handed over our strength, our confidence, our light.

No wonder we feel impoverished without them—we gave them everything we were proud of in ourselves.

Admiration, though, is solid. No magnifier needed here. It's grounded in genuine appreciation for who they are, strengths, flaws and everything in between.

A healthy relationship isn't sunshine and roses, some 100% happiness jet ride into the sky. Life is full of valleys and hills. It works as long as you are both invested in creating a shared space. Sure, there will be high-flying moments and instances in which you'd rather hide... but it's about showing up, even when the ride gets bumpy.

Each person takes charge of their own fulfillment while also cheering on their partner's dream-building efforts. It's great when your partner surprises you with something you wanted, but don't turn these moments into love tests. They are bonuses, not requirements. Enjoy them when they come.

Blame games? Nope, not here. Healthy people say, 'I feel upset when this happens,' instead of, 'You always mess this up.' No finger-pointing or wrestling. Picture a naval strategy table -map spread out, tools in hand- as two commanders meet to plan their next moves, deciding who is best suited to fix the issue while the other steps up with support.

They listen when their partner opens up.

They know it is not a contest, no need to win.

Main goal? Finding a way forward together...

...or stepping back to let the other take action.

No meddling, no hovering.

You shouldn't feel guilty for needing space or expressing what you need, want, or what's acceptable on your terms.

In healthy relationships, everyone gets their private time. If you are on a Zoom call and can't wave hello, your partner doesn't spiral into, "Here we go again, nobody cares about me." Relax. People get busy, and in occasions they just need some personal time.

Build a connection grounded in admiration, respect, and the thrill of surprise. A partnership where you show up fully, rooting for each other with zero half-measures. That's the foundation, the no-fluff kind that doesn't just sound great: It is great.

You each bring your full self -the good, the messy, the mind-itching, no-edits needed. No compromises on who you are. What you get is a bond forged in reality, not fantasy. Refusing to buckle under pressure.

Listen, if someone says "no" to something, that's their freaking freedom of choice. Respect it. In fact, they'll probably respect you more for it. Relationships work when both sides can negotiate a middle ground.

Couples are not conflict-free. Arguments happen, and honestly, they need to! It's a sign of interest. That both of you are trying to navigate each other's imperfections and still stand up for what you believe in.

The key difference is how you handle those arguments. In a healthy dynamic, you tackle the issues without turning it into a personal smackdown. As I said, drop the entitlement to be right all the time, nobody cares. Keep your eyes on what matters, and find (negotiate) a solution that works for both of you.

Let me tell you something that might sound a bit silly and, okay, a little vanilla: my husband and I end every argument by literally taking steps toward each other. Yup, honest, we actually meet in the middle, and we end up laughing. Why? Because here's what happens: when there's a "winner" in the argument, that means there's also a "loser." When that pans out, guess what? The relationship is the real loser.

So instead of going for the knockout punch, aim for a win-win, even if that means an agree to disagree. Match the other person's energy and uplift them. Take those steps toward each other, and you'll find that meeting in the middle is where the wonders really take place.

Lastly, never forget: your partner is not your project. You are not here to fix them, change them, or mold them into your perfect image ...and they shouldn't be doing that to you, either. A healthy relationship accepts each other, quirks and all.

Sure, you grow and evolve together, but it's about supporting each other's growth, not demanding it.

Old Nuclear Family? R.I.P.

Now, here's a reality check: sometimes, even two perfectly healthy people end up in an unhealthy relationship. Why? Because we are all running on that outdated nuclear family chip.

My godmother has a beautiful relationship with her husband. They are both architects who run their business together. Their home feels like a masterpiece of harmony.

Step inside, and you'll find her comfortably seated in the living room. Her husband will greet you with a warm smile and a gentle, "Cup of tea?" or "Cheese and wine?" –depending on the hour. If the phone rings, he's up in a flash to answer it, seamlessly orchestrating every moment.

One day, I asked my godmother how she managed to get him to be so active and involved. I remember her response like it was yesterday. She said:

The day I got married, my grandmother told me:

The first one to take a seat will always ride seated.

That's the nuclear family. It worked, until it didn't. You pour in the passion, give up pieces of yourself, bending over backwards to make it work. Until one day, it starts feeling like a chore instead of an adventure. That's when resentment creeps in, and all that idealization turns into frustration.

It's you, me, and all the sacrifices we make trying to become 'one.' But let's get real, what are we even saying here? It's an impossible fantasy. You are TWO freaking people!

Don't get me wrong, I have nothing against the nuclear family. In fact, I fully support it when it comes to child development. But let's be real, it's R.I.P. as a universal model because society has moved past it.

Fierce, independent women ditching their last names like property on transfer? That patriarchal model was built for a time when rigid roles kept people economically and socially dependent.

Now? It's a shortcut to self-betrayal, a breeding ground for resentment and self-loss.

That outdated structure is crumbling under modern realities, leaving people vulnerable when the illusion of forever shatters.

Ward Cleaver's partners today -no matter what letter they embrace- aren't just waiting at home with a roast in the oven and a martini in hand. They're running businesses, leading teams, making moves. The old model doesn't fit because we've outgrown it. It doesn't protect us, it puts us at risk.

The future? A dynamic where love isn't sacrifice. It's building something greater without shrinking to fit.

You, me, and the relationship. Each a pillar, each essential, none collapsing into the other. That's the core of Binary Relationships Theory, strengthened by the Strategic Emotional Investment Model.

Because love should be a choice, not a trap.

Love should expand you, not shrink you.

Build something real. A relationship that's not just give-and-take, but a true collaboration–one where you both thrive, both invest, and both indulge in your own self-fulfillment.

What shape? Whatever gets you fired up. Feel free to create your own love paradigm: your style, your way.

Healthy couples learn to dance with life. You move together, not scrambled. Sometimes leading, sometimes following, but always keeping the beat. Part of that dance is feeling secure enough to celebrate each other's wins. When your partner shines, you damn well cheer. When you are on top, they're not threatened or overshadowed. And when life knocks you down, they're there, steady and strong, ready to catch the rhythm again. There's enough ground for both of you to stand tall and thrive.

So, how do you spot a healthy one? Find someone who respects both you and themselves, who turns the relationship into a real partnership -not some damn tug-of-war. Look for the one who speaks your life language, who truly gets you. If you both show up, keep that spark alive, and make life an adventure, then hell, you are on the right track.

20- The Reset Roadmap

Before you close this book, I want to leave you with a roadmap.

Maybe you've felt like your world has shattered into a million pieces, and no amount of duct tape is going to fix it. You have replayed the past like it's a bad soap opera, tried to 'find meaning,' and still, nothing. Here is why: you are looking in the wrong place.

My sister, Lilly, and I have faced these same hard truths, and together, we have identified three key realizations:

1. **What broke was never meant to hold you together in the first place**. As I've shown you throughout the book, part of that life was not fully yours to begin with. Think about it: how long were you accommodating to the circumstances, adapting, surviving? Let it go. Start building something new.

2. **Stop staring at the past like it's got answers.** That past is a burned-out GPS. Your answers aren't back there. They are here: now.

3. **That victim mentality? The 'poor me' thing?** Time to RSVP no.

I've told you over and over, if you have a dream, the only solid way to reach it is by driving yourself there. If someone hands it to you, it won't taste or feel the same.

Chasing your dreams is terrifying. That's why the victim mentality is so tempting, while letting you believe it's not your fault. It even gives you the right to complain about how others have failed you. But here's the trap: the more you embrace it, the more it becomes who you are. And strangely enough? Staying stuck starts to feel safer than risking change—or even putting in the effort to chase success.

The truth? No one can pull you out of your hole, except you. People can listen, nod... and still leave you exactly where you are.

Still waiting for a rescue? A sign? A stroke of fate? Stop. No one is coming. You pull yourself out, or you stay stuck. No dreams ever reached. Same story, same ending.

I get it, when pain is your identity, moving forward feels like erasing yourself. But listen: You are not your wounds. You are what comes after them.

So... victim mentality? RSVP, NO!

Betrayal doesn't just break your trust. It devastated the platform of meaning that held your identity and your life together. Since infancy, our sense of self has been supported by others–psychoanalytically speaking, we are born into relational dependence. But at some point, we have to stand on our own. That's how crucial autonomy is.

As I explained in the chapter *Cracking the Code of Betrayal...*, the moment a question mark attaches itself to your memories of the betrayer, and all what you've been to together. Those experiences lose their power as signifiers. They are no longer your anchor. They are just echoes of doubt, uncertainty, and confusion. This is why you feel unmoored and directionless. That is what we need to tackle first.

I will say it another way. Did you know that an ineffective autonomic nervous system response can get stuck in a loop? Instead of adapting, it keeps firing the same reactions. Like a broken record, stuck on the same old script, while everyone else has moved on.

Think about chronic stress or trauma responses. It keeps defaulting to fight, flight, freeze, or fawn, even when the threat is long gone. The body remains hyper-vigilant or shuts down, unable to shift into ease.

Reset breaks that cycle. It's a pattern interrupt, forcing the nervous system to pause and register something different, whether through movement, breath, or sensory shifts. It's the difference between staying overwhelmed, and realizing you could try another way in. Without Reset, the system just keeps spinning its wheels, reinforcing the same ineffective responses.

That's why I created the Reset, Rebuild, and Rise roadmap, to get you out of that mess and back in the driver's seat. Because here's the deal: Nietzsche wasn't just throwing around cool one-liners when he said, "What does not kill you makes you stronger."[26] That should be your damn promise to yourself. Period.

Something I mentioned in a previous chapter as a shift in the logic of how we go about living. That intertwined experience of pleasure and pain that shapes the way we interpret and respond to the world around us: the *jouissance* in Lacanian psychoanalysis. That is what we actually reset after betrayal! Our worldview.

Reset

It begins when you decide -fully, completely- that you've had enough of spinning in circles.

Remember your past experiences, specifically, the ones that shaped your signifiers? Not just who Jay was, but how it felt to be next to Jay Whozit.

---

[26] Nietzsche, Twilight of the Idols, 1888.

Keep in mind, we are working within the binary relationship theory. So, it's not about Jay. It's about your experience of Jay. That's what really counts.

That energy, that pull.

Now? Doesn't it all feel like one big question mark?

Like I said before, when that happens, your past stops holding you the way it used to. Those weren't just memories; they were anchors that shaped your world, the rhythm that made it all make sense.

So what is reset? It's a deep urge. It's a push to step out, to create new anchors, new meaning, new rhythm. A push to create new foundational experiences so your system can recalibrate, and you can find solid ground again.

Think of it this way. You can tell yourself you've moved on all you want, but until your bones, breath, and heartbeat agree, it's just wishful thinking.

True healing isn't about overanalyzing the past. It's about syncing mind and body until you feel the shift.

Reset isn't some grand rational declaration. It's an internal, visceral shift. If betrayal has scrambled your ability to plan and make decisions, trapping you in survival mode, freeze, flight, fight, or fawn (where you appease to avoid further harm). Then, reset is what snaps you out of it.

How? Your nervous system needs a shift: change the question, change the internal context.

Think of preparing for a one-way trip. You are packing your imaginary bags, leaving behind what no longer serves you. What you pack matters. Yet, since you are the one driving, let's make sure you are ready for the road ahead:

Open the windows: Reset starts when you stop living in a sealed-off version of yourself. Open the windows in your house, but more importantly, open your senses. Let new air, new light, and new experiences in. Get curious and step out of the sanctuary of your cave.

Decluttering: Clear out the junk. Both in your space and your mind, because one reflects the other. The day after my sister was betrayed, she woke up, went to the kitchen, and made eggs. Eggs! Then it hit her, she didn't even eat eggs. That was his habit, his breakfast. Clean up the routines that no longer serve you, not just your house.

Breathing: Master those intentional breaths that quiet the chaos and bring you back to center, you are going to need them. Two minutes, just your breath. That's it. No extra gear, no big setup. And bonus? Deep breathing activates your vagus nerve (part of your parasympathetic nervous system), the body's natural calming switch.

Want more? Alternate hot and cold in the shower, or gently place wrapped up ice packs on the back of your neck, especially if tension builds there. These small moves help regulate your system and keep you steady when everything feels like it's spinning.

Rest: Real, deep rest that actually refuels you. Stretch, breathe, and turn off the TV and all your phone apps an hour before bed.

Nourishment: Can you gain clarity and strength on booze and coffee? Of course not! Who are you kidding? Feed your body with power-packed fuel, not comfort food. If your mission is to move forward, then fuel up with purpose.

Movement: Get your body in motion: stretch, walk, or dance like nobody's watching.

All of these things help flip the switch. Here you start breaking free from survival mode, widening your view of life, strengthening the connection to your context, and stepping into clarity one move at a time.

Notice something? Nothing is forced. It's all natural. Release the control and dive in.

When I was 11 years old, I went sailing with my parents to Brazil. One night, the pampero winds came. If you've never heard of them, pamperos are furious winds that rip through the ocean at over 70mph without warning, leaving disarray in their wake.

That night, we had more than one pampero shredding every sail on our boat like it was paper. I can still see my mother sewing as fast as her hands could move, and my father hauling up the next sail, only to watch it rip apart too.

The waves towered over us like giants, and our boat– a 32-foot sailboat- felt like a nutshell in an endless, angry ocean. Then came the moment I'll never forget. My father called us to check the food and water reserve. He got the dinghy ready, the small lifeboat we would use if the worst happened.. and that only gets ready when the sailing boat is about to go down.

My mother stopped sewing. She carefully walked through the tilting cabin, swaying with the rocking waves. I watched her grab her medicine bag. Then she came back to me, holding out a Valium. That was her way of protecting me. If the worst was to come, at least being sedated not to suffer as everything around us seemed to be falling apart.

But storms, as violent as they are, don't last forever. Just as quickly as it came, the pampero left. We were surrounded by stillness, miles of ocean on all sides. No land. No GPS to tell us where to go. Nothing but my father's sextant and the stars.

We had no idea where we were, but we knew we had to reset. It started with the basics: figuring out our location, tending to our bodies, and trusting the tools we had. From there, we could rebuild our plan and chart a course forward.

Betrayal is no different. More than leaving you stranded, it rips up your damn map. Tosses your compass overboard, and leaves you wondering if you'll ever find land again.

But listen: You don't need to know exactly where you are to start. You just need to take the first step, reconnect with your body, and trust that your internal compass ...yes, the one you've been doubting, that one will get you through.

That's how recovery begins, not by scrambling to fix the fragmented pieces of what's left or retracing old steps, but by tuning into yourself and knowing, deep down, that you are done feeling hurt.

Pressing reset is shifting your focus toward positive actions that feel aligned, inside out. Those will pull you out of the hole and into something productive.

Rebuild

This is where the magic happens. Rebuild is your shift from just getting by to creating a life you are excited to wake up to every day.

Patching up old wounds won't cut it. Recovery after betrayal requires building something new and stepping into a future where you call the shots.

Here's how we'll do it:

Awakening: Reconnect with your senses and the world around you. Notice the little things, the breeze on your skin, the sound of your favorite song. These small moments anchor you in the present and open doors to new possibilities.

Reframing: Shift your mindset. You'll start seeing yourself, your life, and your choices through a new lens. Every action, every habit, will align with the future you are creating.

Autonomy: Own your choices. Align with your purpose. This is where you take back control and start living life on your terms, no more playing by someone else's rules.

Rebuild is about momentum. Brick by brick, choice by choice, you are creating a foundation that's unshakable.

That alignment? It doesn't happen in your head. It happens in motion, in action, in new experiences that overwrite those old and cracked signifiers we've talked about. That's how you rebuild meaning.

So, stop caving, drop the damn phone, and the everlasting TikTok show...All that: gone!

Absorb life.

The fullness of it.

Because that's where your healing power is. That's how you come back to yourself, by building forward.

Remember when I said, 'Stop staring at the past like it's got answers'? That wasn't just a throwaway line. It's the truth. Clarity comes from anchoring yourself in the present and letting your body guide you -deciding what to keep, what to release, and what is your next move. Rebuilding through embodiment is how you make meaning from the inside out.

As the foundation of small wins, this is where you learn to move through your life with intention. From now on, every action, every choice, becomes a brick in the foundation of your new self.

Some days, you'll feel unstoppable.

Other days... like you are dragging your feet through wet cement.

All that is normal. What matters is that you keep moving.

Here's the fascinating part: every small, intentional step you take rewires your brain. This process, called neuroplasticity, strengthens the pathways that support confidence and trust, making the new you feel more natural with every move, each brick you lay. Pair those steps with sensory awareness, and your brain starts associating action with stability and growth.

So, speak up.

Go for a walk.

Play with your dog or climb up a tree.

Try something new.

Slowly, through Neural Pathway Activation and Sensory Reframing Techniques, you are building a framework for a future that feels steady, aligned, and undeniably yours.

Slowly the pieces of your effort come together. Bold steps, small wins, responsibility and purposeful action stack into something real.

Rise

The process does not end here. This is that serendipitous moment when you look back and realize, *'What the heck... I did that!?'* A celebratory aha moment that, right now, might feel impossible.

You start to see it in the life you've created, whether it's a family, a hobby, a business, or simply the ability to face the world with a fearless heart.

Betrayal has forced you to question every step that led you here. It stripped away the layers of who you once were,... and even more, the version of yourself you thought you had to be. You see the moments you blended in, conformed, forgave, and forgot... just to fit, just to keep everything looking pristine while your heart took the blows. Then, it hits you:

betrayal didn't break you.

It showed you who you are.

It didn't define you, it ignited you.

You rose, not in spite of the pain, but because of it. And with every step forward, you shaped something greater than what was lost. You turned the wreckage into your masterpiece.

This is your rise.

Not just survival, but transformation.

Bold. Unshaken. Untouchable. Because this time, what you've built? No storm can take it down.

21- Rise & Shine. Show Them What You Were Hiding Beneath All That Sacrificing

Can you see it now? You are not that same person that a few years ago, running across the street, still in med school, wind snatching your papers, playing matchmaker like it was your side hustle.

You've spent years making sure everyone else is set, handled, taken care of. And yet, here you are, doubting yourself? Well, in my book, if you can orchestrate everyone else's life like a pro ....imagine what happens when you turn that energy toward yourself!

That power? It's always been yours.

Oh, yes. Betrayal has a way of making you second-guess it.

You saw the red flags. You felt the gut punches. You had moments when you wanted to scream the truth but swallowed it instead... All to keep the peace, to hold it together, to push forward. And now? That silence, that effort, is buried under the weight of grudges you don't even realize are dragging you down.

Can you see it now? The whole damn thing. The betrayal, yes. But also the part you played. The bending, swallowing, forgetting and denying, the sacrificing, and all what falls under self-betrayal.

You did it for love.

But now? Now it's time to love yourself. Because if self-betrayal got you here, self-loyalty will pull you out.

I handed you the tools... The move? That's always been yours.

We've tackled love dynamics, the binary relationship theory, and even broken down how to share the same roof without losing it and what to do about the kids. Admit it, your toolkit got heavier, right? You can talk about the signifier like a professor and spot waxies and Machiavellians from a mile away.

But more important than watching who surrounds you, the biggest lesson here is this: betrayal wasn't meant to trap you in a suffocating blanket of wrath.

It came to dismantle you, so you could break free. Free from the cocoon of self-imposed emotional contortions, obligations, and denials that held together that castle in the air you worked so hard to maintain.

So please, don't convince yourself that sacrificing everything for the kids is different from what you did for your partner. It's not. Same story, different excuse.

Let's be honest, that's just fear talking. Fear of standing fully in your own power. Fear of claiming a life that is yours, and finding yourself alone in it.

Here's the truth: all this time, the one thing you ever had to do was stand tall and true.

It's not selfish.

Your strength, your love, your health, and your happiness don't take away from those around you.

They make everyone better.

Divorce? Staying together? That's your call. Your life, your rules. What I've been saying from the very first chapter and all the way through is this: learn how to love. Because love isn't just about feelings; it's a structure. A three-element relationship, and it comes with conditions. Feelings may spark the relationship, but it's our agreements that sustain it. That's where negotiations happen, where maturity kicks in.

...And autonomy? It's what turns you into a master at dealing those terms, instead of just accepting whatever's thrown your way.

It's your call. And only you can feel when it's time.

Close your eyes for a moment. Picture a balloon in your hands. Feel its surface, smooth and rubbery, stretched tight with everything inside it.

Take a deep breath and blow into it.

With every breath, you push out your frustrations, your pains, your heartbreaks. Watch the balloon swell, expanding with everything you've been holding in. Every disappointment, every betrayal... let it fill.

Keep going until there's nothing left to pack inside.

Now, hold it for a moment. Feel the weight of what you've carried. And when you are ready. When you know you are ready, take a deep breath... and pop it. Gone.

Just like that.

No more holding, no more carrying.

That weight? Gone.

That energy? Yours again.

Because that's one of the two things you need to do today: forgive, reclaim your energy. And now, the second one...

Close this book and face forward.

Life doesn't wait. It moves, and so do you.

This book has been your guide.

Next move is yours.

Show the world what you are really made of!!

Your Survival Toolkits

A- The Post-Breakup Survival Guide

You've made it this far. Before we focus on tackling co-parenting, legal battles, or the emotional whirlwind, you need to get yourself together.

Remember? You had plans. Big ones. Maybe med school, launching a business, or simply waking up every morning knowing exactly who you were and what you wanted.

...And then? Life happened. Love happened. You compromised, and forgiving, forgetting, and learning not to see, you also carried the weight.

You don't owe anyone the version of you that keeps shrinking to make them comfortable. The moment you let go, step out of the cycle of betrayal and start believing in yourself, that post-split glow will find you.

That glow isn't just about looking good. It's what happens when you remember who you are. The quiet confidence that appears when you stop asking for permission to take up space. The energy that radiates and makes people wonder what changed. The answer? You did.

That glow? It's proof you are rebuilding from the inside out.

The moment you start shining, it's time to handle the practical side of freedom. Now, if divorce is even a whisper in your head, your first move better be locking down a few things:

First off, make sure you have health insurance. Don't get left out in the cold. Start researching your options. If you are under your partner's health insurance, check how divorce could affect your coverage. Otherwise, consider private insurance, whatever it takes to stay covered. Not exactly a thrill ride, yet absolutely essential.

Next, get yourself a skill, specially if it's been a hot minute since you were working. Time to make sure you have something to fall back on. Be smart about it. Skip the debt. Pick a course, take a workshop, grab a certificate, or tap into career coaching. Upgrade your resume, and get back out there with something solid in hand. Start turning those talents into dollar signs!

Got a degree collecting dust with zero real-world action? Wake it up! Find a place you'd love to work, get your foot in the door by volunteering, and let that be your stepping stone to a full-time gig.

Before you go full steam ahead, let's talk stealth.

If you are not ready to drop hints yet, keep things quiet. Be smart about every move. Open accounts, update documents, and make changes discreetly. This is not the time to leave breadcrumbs.

I'm not here to scare you, but here is the reality, in the U.S., intimate partners are responsible for nearly half of female homicide victims, 10% of male homicides, and 6%[27] suicides. This isn't something to take lightly. If you can, avoid doing this alone. Lean on trusted friends, family, or professionals to help steady the path ahead.

Now, let's talk cash and financial independence.

Step one: *Build. That. Credit.* Got a bank account only in both of your names? Open your own. Like, now. Go online, start an account, and snag a credit card in your name. It takes five minutes online, and bam! ...you are already ahead of the game.

In the meantime... Do you have a life insurance policy? Estate plans? It's time to make some changes. Put in who you want. Change the beneficiaries and revise your will. I know it's hard, and it might feel bad to think in these terms, but you must protect your future.

Let's not forget to get copies of tax returns, property deeds, bank statements ...the lot! You don't want to be piecing things together last minute. Know what you

---

[27] Statistics from AbiNader, Graham & Kafka, 2023.

own, what you owe, and where it all stands. This is your financial foundation.

Remember, you are not protecting what you now have. You are laying the groundwork to build the life you deserve. One step at a time, you are making space for something better.

As you are getting closer to D Day (Departure), double down on privacy and security. This isn't the time for half-measures. Lock it down like Fort Knox, because if you think for one second your partner isn't capable of a little "digital check-in," think again.

Take a hard look at every device you own, computer, phone, tablet, smartwatch, even that smart speaker eavesdropping in the corner. Does your dog have a smart collar? Even your car tracks where you've been, don't overlook it. Make sure they aren't secretly sending your info out like some kind of open diary.

Turn off location sharing like it's the plague. Every app, every device... if it's tracking, it's off. You are nobody's dot on a map.

Go nuclear on passwords: bank accounts, emails, social media, even YouTube, especially if you have been getting smart on it. Every last one, and make them a bit challenging. Toss in symbols, mix up cases, and if possible, add a space—yes, a space! Make ‘em sweat if they even think about messing with your stuff.

Then, grab anything personal, valuable, or sentimental that belongs to you, and stash it somewhere only you can access. If it’s not marital property, it’s secure. A friend’s house, a lockbox—whatever makes it untouchable.

Finally, don’t even think about leaving shared devices in play. Log out, wipe ‘em clean, hit factory reset. Whatever it takes. This is your life and your privacy, and you are the only one who gets full access.

Are you afraid of your betrayer? What are the safe zones in your house? If you start a discussion, walk towards these areas or -if possible- get out towards the street. Avoid the kitchen, the stairway, and any other place more prone to accidents.

Keep a friend, a family member in the loop. Also, if possible, don’t feel ashamed and have a good neighbor informed of your situation in case you need to get out of your home in a rush.

Keep a change of clothes for you and your children, and all your documents accessible. If the police shows up, get their names and badges and take note of all the witnesses around you.

During the peaceful moments alone with your kids, crank up the music. Sing, dance, and let loose with your kids. Those bursts of joy? They are like a breath of fresh air when things are heavy. They help you and your kids bond and work through emotions together. Plus, it beats zoning out in front of the TV or listening to music solo, which only makes you all feel more disconnected. The best part? You are creating lasting, happy memories right in the middle of all the commotion.

Tip: Years ago, I had a client who was extremely afraid of her husband. She hid an AirTag in his car to get notifications whenever he was in close proximity.

Be aware that in many places, walking away from your shared home under the "abandonment" doctrine could mess with your property rights. What does that mean? You might end up stuck coexisting with the person who betrayed you until the court or another type of formal agreement sorts things out. Tough situation, I know... but check the Quick & Dirty Coexistence Survival Toolkit, or go to my website and check all the different very useful tools at your fingertips.

B- Here's Your Checklist To Call It Out

Now that you are handling the logistics of moving forward, let's talk about two essential pieces: how betrayal has actually hit you, and how the roles you tend to play around the binary space might be keeping you stuck.

If you don't recognize the damage, it's easy to stay reactive instead of actually healing. And if you can't see how these roles interact, you might miss the deeper reason why stepping fully in (or fully out) matters.

When you are standing at the edge, thinking you are protecting yourself from another heartbreak, you might actually be sliding into an even greater risk without realizing it.

Remember that hamster-wheel cycling?

Yeap. Let's not do that.

Been there, done that.

Here's your checklist based on what most people feel after betrayal. As you go through it, ask yourself: when did these feelings first show up? Was it before or after the betrayal? Some of them may tie back to earlier pain, not just this moment. Take it easy. Be honest, and see what hits home...

Guarded Behavior: You have built walls around your heart, wary and watchful, no longer taking words at face value, shielding yourself from unseen strikes.

Loss of Trust: Struggling to find confidence in others and in your own judgments.

Anxiety and Depression: Worrying too much, being afraid of the next let down, or having persistent feelings of sadness or hopelessness. Unable to enjoy the hobbies and activities you once loved.

Emotional Distance and Estrangement: Pulling away emotionally from the person who betrayed you or, even, from others in general as a way to protect yourself. See Guarded Behavior' above.

Reduced Intimacy: Intimacy is out the window. It's so hard to let the wall down and allow yourself to connect with people. Perhaps casual sex becomes an alternative, but it's a meaningless one.

Anger: You are engulfed in a blaze of anger, directed both at the one who betrayed you and at yourself for not seeing the storm coming.

Withdrawal: The comfort zone of your personal cave becomes your kingdom, thank goodness for Zoom!

Avoidance: Conscious or unconscious efforts to not deal with a stressor in order to protect yourself.

Obsessive Thinking: Engaging in repetitive and intrusive thoughts about the betrayal, often replaying the event or seeking answers to unanswered questions.

Difficulty Coping: You are drowning in a pool of emotions and tasks so deep that at times it takes a toll on your body, and you are pretty good at hiding this.

Hyper-vigilance: You are constantly on the lookout, scanning for any hint of betrayal or dishonesty in new and existing relationships, always on guard.

Difficulty building relationships: Struggling with attachment issues, finding it challenging to form new relationships or to manage the ones you have in a secure and healthy way.

Self-Doubt: You are caught in a storm of self-questioning, wondering if you somehow caused the betrayal, questioning your worth in every glance.

Isolation: You feel stranded on an island of your experience, unable to find anyone who truly understands the sea you are navigating.

Physical Symptoms: Your body echoes the chaos of your mind with headaches, stomachaches, and tense muscles, the physical toll of emotional turmoil.

Sleep Disturbances: Nights are restless, haunted by nightmares of betrayal, leaving you more entangled in anxiety and distress.

Loss of sense of Identity: You feel like a stranger to yourself. The betrayal cracked your self-image, and now you are unsure who's looking back in the mirror.

Boundary Struggles: You are setting boundaries believing it will keep you safe, just because you will spot and deem a boundary violator to anyone crossing that line.

Seeking Reassurance: You are on a quest for validation, constantly seeking signs that you are still wanted, still valued and not truly believing the answers you are given.

Emotional Numbing: You shield yourself from pain, retreating into numbness. Which one are you: locking yourself away in silence or drowning in uproar, filling the void with people, reckless encounters, compulsive sex? Chasing a high that never truly dulls the ache?

You think you are escaping, but you are just trading one kind of suffering for another. The body remembers. The mind knows, ...and beneath it all, a part of you is still waiting to be heard.

Concentration Difficulties: Your focus is scattered, hijacked by intrusive thoughts and the shadow of betrayal that looms over you.

Loss of Faith: Trust in relationships feels like a bridge burned, leaving you skeptical of love's very possibility.

Mood Swings: You are riding a rollercoaster of emotions, from depths of despair to peaks of anger, battling a whirlwind within.

Escapism: Reality feels too sharp, so you lose yourself in daydreams, games, work, or anything that dulls the edge of your pain.

Heightened Sensitivity: Every reminder of the betrayal is a live wire, sparking intense emotional reactions.

Self-Blame: You shoulder the betrayal as if it were your own doing, carrying a burden that was never yours to bear.

Reconnecting Difficulties: The chasm between you and the one who betrayed you seems too wide, trust and intimacy eroded to dust.

Fear of Abandonment: The ghost of betrayal follows you, whispering fears of being left behind again, leading to desperate grips on those around you.

Cynicism Towards Love: Love, to you, now wears a cloak of skepticism, seen as a fairytale with a grim ending.

Long-Term Scars: Yes, the betrayal might have left indelible marks, scars that may shape your heart and relationships long into the future. It doesn't have to be this way.

How many did you count? More than five? Seven? Now, think about how much these symptoms are affecting you. How big of a deal are they in your daily life?

Minimal: I still do my thing, no problem.

Moderate: I've missed a few days of work this month, I can't concentrate, and I've checked off about a third of what's listed.

Severe: I can't do most of what needs to get done. I'm dragging myself out of bed, low on energy, and my mind's still a blur. Plus, I'm ticking off more than half of what you listed.

If you are finding yourself in the moderate or severe category, don't go through it alone. Reach out.

You are Not a Character, You are the Author

Time to go back to those emotional roles we fall into—The Hero, The Martyr, The Ghost...—and how they operate within the binary space.

These aren't just personality quirks; they're positions in a system. Think of them less as traits and more like functions: reflective, transitive, asymmetrical, or even destructive. At the beginning of life we enter the shared emotional field carrying those patterns, and from there on they keep us on the loop.

Bellow is the chart, but let's break it down as a felt experience.

The Fixer: They rush into the space with one mission: to solve. But solving is their way of not collapsing. Their identity depends on things staying broken enough to fix, so they can feel useful... but not so broken as to overwhelm them.

The Martyr: They shrink to keep the peace. It's hard for them to see options, because they work overtime hoping that if they give enough, endure enough, it will finally earn them love. But all they're doing is merging into their partners: Identity collapse disguised as devotion.

The Hero: They don't just perform strength—they curate it. They take pride in doing what's right, holding things together, and proving they're dependable. But their presence is performance.

They want to be admired more than known.

Respected more than reached.

And they always need someone orbiting them. Someone effective, functional, emotionally available, to make them feel whole.

Role	Function Type	Symbolic Placement
The Hero	*Asymmetrical*	Dominates the relationship space
The Martyr	*Self-sacrificial*	Collapses self into Other
The Orbiter	*Reflective*	Defines self only through Other
The Ghost	*Nullifier*	Attacks or evades the relationship
The Fixer	*Transitive*	Tries to fix or be useful Self→Other/Relationship
The Collector	*Non-differentiated*	Blurs boundaries across all connections
The "Unconditional" Lover	*Contractual / Paradoxical*	Demands certainty while denying expectations

The Ghost: Quiet. Distant. Detached. They exit without a trace, sometimes physically, often emotionally. They may look cool. Untouched. But for them, connecting the dots between head and heart feels impossible. This isn't just emotional unavailability. It's what psychoanalyst Wilfred Bion called an attack on the link, an inability to bind thoughts to feelings, to bind feelings to people.

The Ghost doesn't just disappear from relationships. They disappear from meaning. They'd rather dissolve the bond than risk being transformed by it.

Each of these roles is a function in the emotional system.

The Fixer reflects what's broken.

The Martyr absorbs what's missing, carrying the weight no one asked them to hold.

The Hero performs strength, order, control... while hiding their own need to be seen.

And the Ghost? The Ghost disappears, because connection feels like risk.

These aren't personality flaws. They're trauma strategies, wrapped in love costumes. Emotional contracts we never consciously signed up for, and that we replay, again and again, inside the relationship space.

Until you name the role.

Until you step out of it.

Until you show up: Not as a function, but as a person.

In the Binary Space, there are always three elements:

Self (Person A)

Other (Person B)

And the shared emotional field: the "relationship."

For example, let's say a couple is made up of a Fixer and a Martyr. The Fixer's identity depends on the relationship staying broken enough to keep fixing, but not so broken they feel helpless. They present themselves as the helper, the one holding things together. Don't get allured by their compensation. Underneath, many times they are the ones who actually need rescuing.

Figure: Fixer & Martyr, two survival roles driven by the same undercurrent: "*If I stop performing, will you still want me?*"

Wish to be recgonized, performs through sacrifice:
"*Look how much I've endured for you*"

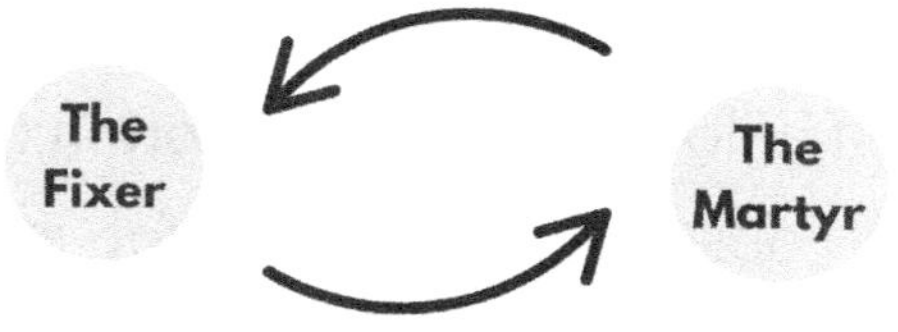

Wish to be useful, performs through action:
"*Let me make it better for you.*"

Meanwhile, the Martyr adapts endlessly, bending until they vanish. They don't ask for much, because their worth is tied to how much they can endure—even if they complain all day long. That's their love call. They believe that sacrifice and working hard somehow will magically fix everything.

What happens when a Fixer and a Martyr pair up?

One person self-erases.

The other avoids collapse by constantly working to "save" something, while hiding their own need to be saved.

But nothing heals.

Because if it did, the Fixer would lose their purpose. The Martyr would have to risk taking full command of their own life, rather than living through someone else's. And without the roles? Love becomes terrifyingly real.

I call it an excuse. Not as judgment, but because that's how it feels:

As long as I'm needed, I'm worthy.

If I'm useful, I must be lovable.

And that loop? It's not love. It's emotional reenactment on repeat. You won't find saving -or solving- here. Stop stepping into the relationship space like you are there to get something.

The relational space isn't the problem. It becomes a stage when you enter as anyone else but yourself. So,...

Drop the role.

Claim your agency.

And Walk in tall to rewrite your damn story.

That shift? Game changer.

Because when you step into the binary space with presence, clarity, and self-respect, you stop the loop cold. It's not about creating a story that will make you feel whole:

Show up first.

Stand in your damn truth.

Write from there.

Embody your life. Because you don't need to be fixed to take space.

C- Get some Me Time!

Welcome! Good to know you can take five for some 'me time.'

Did you get to read, 'Cracking the Code'? and the 'Reset Roadmap'?

Take a breather.

...Hell, head to the kitchen, or better yet, step outside and bring along that drink you were having, whether it was your caffeine fix or something with a little more kick, you need it.

Did you catch that part about how we never truly see reality in its raw form... until it hits us? In the meantime, whatever doesn't fit or feels off, we just override it with logic. Honestly, that's a smart move... until it isn't.

I truly believe in the wisdom of Mother Nature. Those so-called red flags? We ignore them because we're not ready to face them ...it's too damn risky.

Those red flags were warnings, and now you are finally in a place where you can do something about it.

Things unravel when they are supposed to, not a second earlier. When Mother Nature brings them in, it means you've got Her backing. It means you have the power to overcome this.

Of course, some people have perfected denial, while others are experts at playing the victim. You could have kept pushing forward, eyes tightly shut, pretending everything's fine. But who were you kidding?

So, thumbs up for choosing the blue pill and reading this book.

You've dropped the act.

You've stepped out of the grind.

You are here because you want back your good nights of sleep. Because you want space to breathe, to unknot that throat that's been holding you tight.

Now, get ready to dive in a bit more. These questions aren't here to coddle you. They are here to shake things up and help you rebuild your story. No sugar-coating, just bold truth. It's time to get back in the game.

Flip that page and start crafting the next chapter of your life.

Make it bold.

Make it count.

Build your masterpiece.

1-***First up, what are the non-negotiables?*** What do you absolutely need in your life to feel like you? And, on the flip side, what's draining you? What's got to go?

Must Haves	Must Avoids

2- ***What's your spark?*** What made you feel proud, alive, or strong before the betrayal? Think about those moments when you stood tall or felt unstoppable. Now ask yourself: what part of that is not associated with your betrayer? What part of that strength or joy is still within you, waiting to be rediscovered? What's one small step you could take today to bring that back into your life, on your terms?

3- ***Next, What does a healthy, fulfilling relationship look like to you?*** Close your eyes and picture it, not just the person, but the energy and connection between you two. What does it feel like when you are both nurturing the relationship as its own entity, that third element?

4- ***Now, how does your current relationship compare?*** Stack it up against your ideal. Is it aligned? Are you thriving together or just surviving? Be honest, are you both showing up for the relationship itself, or has that third element been left behind?

5- ***What are the deal-breakers for you in this relationship, and have they been crossed?*** It's time to know your non-negotiables. If those lines have been crossed, ask yourself: *What's keeping me here?*

6- ***If fear wasn't holding you back, what would you do?*** Imagine fear has no power over you. What bold move would you make to step fully into this relationship ...or fully out of it?

7- ***What are you sacrificing by staying undecided about your marriage?*** Tick-tock! What's slipping through your fingers while you stay on pause?

8- ***What are the benefits of moving on?*** Freedom? Peace? A fresh start? Take a moment to weigh in on what's on the other side of decision.

9-***Now, think about this:*** if a dear friend were in the same situation as you, what would you ask them? What question would help them see things more clearly? Sometimes, we find the answers we need when we step into someone else's shoes.

10- ***Now flip it:*** imagine it's your child going through this. What would you tell them?

11- ***What sparks your envy?*** Envy isn't just about wishing for what others have, it's a flashing sign pointing to what matters to you. What do you see that stirs something in you? Is it confidence? Adventure? A sense of purpose? A certain lifestyle? Instead of brushing it off, get curious. What's it revealing about what you want more of in your own life? And what's stopping you from making it yours?

D- Quick & Dirty Coexistence Survival Toolkit

Stuck under the same roof for a while? No problem, I got you.

Not stuck?

Well, lucky you! Ok, lets the rest of us figure out how to turn this wreck of a lifeboat into something a little less dramatic… or read it anyway and spread the wisdom.

As promised, bellow is the no-BS rules of propriety to keep things civil (and keep you from losing it). You deserve a space that's at least semi-sane.

If you can, don't settle for less!

…and remember, respect those rules yourself, too.

You want to stay on the court's good side, and the last thing you need is to give them any ammo that could hurt your chances with the kids.

Use this as a starting point and tweak it to fit your needs and lifestyle. For example, you might want to settle who's fixing that picture frame that got knocked over last time things got heated.

A few points before you start scribbling down:

Understand Your Legal Standing: Know your legal rights before making any decisions or signing anything. Always read the fine print yourself. And if something doesn't make sense? Ask. No shame, no hesitation. It's better to be safe than legally trapped.

Manage Your Interactions: It is entirely up to you how much exchange you are comfortable with. Designate neutral zones, like the entryway, the living room, where any brief engagement remains civil. Whether or not you share a meal with your betrayer should be dictated by your sense of emotional safety and how secure you feel at the moment.

Prioritize Emotional Support: Lean on your squad -whether it's supportive friends, family, or professionals- because emotional backup is key right now. Don't hesitate to ask for help; you don't have to go through this solo.

Keep Documentation: Keep a record of every interaction, expenses, agreements, witnesses, police and social workers visit and any other record about your cohabitation. It can be a lifesaver for future disputes or legal drama. If you actually manage to work as a team, good accounts make good friends.

If your betrayer left you with bruises, document them by seeing a doctor right away. Sadly, in this age of Ai, photos alone might not cut it anymore for proving injuries. Get those medical records; they carry way more weight.

Ok, ready?

Thought you were ready? Turns out, one of you is as hard to pin down. Sitting down to hash this out feels like scaling Mount Impossible? Don't panic, you've made it through tougher stuff. It actually buys you time to get ready. You can work things out on your own first and come back with a game plan.

Of course, when one of you sketches it all out solo... it doesn't work as smoothly as when both of you are on board. Yeah, the follow-through won't stick.

Time to break it down and paddle through this mess with your dignity intact. We might not achieve perfection, but we can still make this dinghy livable until one of you finds a better shore:

Whether it's a strict schedule or a rotating deal, the key is to stay reasonable but firm. Protect your space and keep the drama to a minimum!

1. Who's Paying for the Roof Over Our Heads?

Let's get real: money talks, and rent (or mortgage) doesn't pay itself. Lights, water, internet... these are the basics of not turning into medieval peasants. Are we splitting it 50-50, basing it on income, or factoring in who's picking up the tab for other things like food, kids' clothes, or the endless list of life expenses? Are we keeping a shared account just for this? Whatever the plan, write it down and stick to it, because nobody wants a monthly screaming match over who paid what.

...and let's avoid "oops, I forgot to pay the electric bill" sabotage.

2. Fridge Wars: How Do We Divide and Conquer Groceries?

Are we pooling resources like a cooperative commune or living like roommates who barely say hi? Will the fridge have "his and hers" shelves? And what about the last slice of pizza ...are we writing names on it, or is it fair game? Let's avoid passive-aggressive Post-its, shall we?

3. Space: The Final Frontier

Personal space is sacred, and we are not just talking about the bathroom. You are calling the shots here, so make sure to negotiate the vibe that fits your comfort level.

Who's sleeping where? Which corners of the house are private havens, and which are shared battlegrounds? Are common spaces a free-for-all, or do you need a schedule to avoid awkward encounters? How do you want to handle this? How do you want to walk into the house–say hi, or say nothing at all? Are you having two piles of dirty dishes, or keeping the kitchen pristine 24/7?

Whether you break bread together or not? What it comes to interaction, it's *entirely* in your hands. But make sure the rules are clear and agreed on by both of you, based on your comfort and safety. Don't leave it up for guessing. Your life, your rules.

4. How Do We Know When This Chapter Ends?

What happens if the agreement stops working, life gets messy, or something needs to change? Set a plan for how to call for adjustments so that the..."That doesn't work for me," is not a way to dodge responsibility. Nail down the details. Future you will thank you for skipping the headaches.

Yes, this is part of that agreement you both know you need (even if you hate to admit it). It's a no-nonsense playbook that tackles the basics head-on—no fluff, no guessing. Because let's be real: respectful coexistence is your ticket to sanity, a serious energy boost, and staying anchored in what truly matters.

E- CO-PARENTING PLAYBOOK

Ok folks, let's talk about the elephant in the room: you are not a couple anymore, but you are still a team. Why? Because you've got kids who didn't sign up for this drama.

This isn't about your grudges or bruised egos. It's about raising the next generation without dragging them through your mess.

Your goal is to get these kids to handle the divorce like champs? That starts with you. Set the example. Focus on what really matters: giving them stability while staying true to yourself.

So, here is the big question: Years ago, you decided to bring this child into the world. Now ask yourself:

Are you ready to fully take on that responsibility?

...Or are you okay with leaving their future to chance, letting society, social media, or the loudest voice in the room shape their path? The choice is yours. But make no mistake, no one else can play your part.

I will remind you that between going nice or dirty, you chose to go nice on this one. Which means you are your kiddos' best cheerleaders. Don't just say you are a team, prove it. Actions speak louder than words, and your kids will remember how you both show up, even when you don't get along.

No one is expecting co-parents to be best friends, but be considerate of each other. Make things happen, no excuses. That's what counts.

Even if you get divorced, you continue being parents. You are not required to share an address to feel you are a family. What makes a family?

It's not just the people.

It's the relationships between them.

And that third element–the relationship itself– is a living presence.

Family connections come with their own rules of engagement. Many are unspoken, but they are real. Whether under the same roof or towns apart, it continues to come with expectations, rhythms, and emotional agreements.

At the center of it all is what I call the binary space. A living emotional field that holds the bond between everyone involved.

This space isn't just symbolic, it's structural.
The binary space carries weight. And even after a separation, it still deserves basic civility, even if you and your ex can't see eye to eye.

You don't have to like each other.

You are not here to be friends.

Your job is to be team players, with one clear goal in mind: raising those kids in a healthy way.

Your job is to protect that space, because your kids depend on it to grow up with confidence.

Kids don't need a picture-perfect setup; they need a healthy relational space that makes them feel safe and loved. Sometimes, that means two houses. Guess what? That is totally okay, as long as the co-parenting relationship stays steady and respectful.

Now, let me ask you this: if you ate something toxic, would you try to digest it or spit it out? Exactly. Holding onto a toxic dynamic only poisons the well.

You don't have to swallow resentment and dysfunction just to keep up appearances. What matters is making sure your kids grow up seeing a relationship that's healthy, even if it looks different than you first imagined.

Your kids will thrive more with parents who keep things healthy while living apart, rather than being stuck in a house overflowing with tension and lacking in love.

So, smooth up and bring up your best face game.

This is about setting the tone for your kids, not unloading your frustration.

As I was telling you before, at the core of it all is respect.

If kids don't learn to respect their parents, they won't respect anyone

...including themselves.

Respect isn't about fear or obedience. It's about recognizing the value in others, and in yourself.

It's what shapes how we speak, listen, and show up for one another. It's about modeling self-worth and honoring each other's space, time, and truth. Without it, things lose their meaning and everything falls apart. And what's left? Confusion, entitlement, or shaky self-esteem.

The Talk

First of all, you need to bring the news. Before you sit down with the kids, you and your partner need to have a no-nonsense talk. Get on the same page about what you'll say and how you'll handle the big stuff: housing, school, friends, the whole shebang. This isn't couples therapy, it's a strategy meeting for the kids. Ditch the blame and drama.

Whichever the age, the main message is simple: "You'll still see both of us, we both love you, and we're here for you." Period. This is about them, not your baggage. Time to listen.

If things start getting heated, pause. Take a breath, cool down, and remember: this conversation is all about making your kids feel safe, taken care and to discuss living arrangements. That's the mission. Re-focus, and stick to it!

If blame starts to creep in, gently guide the conversation back on track. Have a keyword to alert each other if you are stepping into edgy waters. This can help keep the conversation stay constructive and prevent things from escalating.

Different ages, different approaches.

You might be surprised and find some kids actually feel relieved, especially if they've been stuck in the middle of nonstop conflict at home. Some remain quiet, others feel upset or, worse, guilty, I mean like they think it's their job to fix things, which we both know is not their responsibility.

That's why your top priority is making sure your kids feel safe and loved by both of you, and that they see you both acting as a team. No matter what's happened in the past or what the future holds, this should always be the main message. If I'm repeating myself, it's because this is that important.

By the way, love always comes with limits. Your job as parents isn't just to love. It's to raise strong, capable kids who can handle whatever life throws their way. Because eventually you will not be there to protect and facilitate their wishes.

Anyhow, going back... Whatever your children's response, make sure to give them space to express their feelings and address their concerns with patience and without pressure. Be objective and use a calm, reassuring tone that shows your kids you have got this, despite the fact that you are still figuring out the details. Do not worry about not having answers, because that is not only totally normal it is absolutely okay.

You don't need to have all the answers to be in control

You just need to stay present.

Don't dump your financial drama or other grown-up decisions on them, those aren't theirs to figure out. But do listen to their concerns, and absolutely give them some say in decisions that affect their own life. Especially if they are teenagers, let them have a little control in a few things that matter to them.

I mentioned it before, stop the projection of your guilt and sorrows onto them. That whole 'grieving process' speech? Needs to go. Your kids still have both parents, just new arrangements. They don't need to grieve, they need to adapt. When they are left to do so, they can be damn good at it.

Constantly talking about grief or prepping them for emotional fallout? That's a self-fulfilling prophecy waiting to happen. The moment you act like something should feel broken, you plant the idea. What if they don't feel that way? They might start wondering if something's wrong with them.

...and bam! There it is, your beautiful self-fulfilling prophecy in full, messy, avoidable splendor.

Your guilt? Your sorrow? That's yours to own, not theirs to carry.

..and be careful with guilt!

Guilt is tricky. Sure, it's practically a parenting trademark, but if you let it take the wheel, it can drive you straight into manipulation.... And believe me, that's never going to lead to healthy shores.

While this might be one of the most overwhelming times in your life, try, really try, not to behave in a way that makes others see you as the problem.

If emotions are running high and the police show up, remember this: they don't know who's who. They are stepping into a tense situation, making split-second judgments, and their top priority is keeping the peace and protecting all present, including themselves.

The person who looks the most agitated? The one raising their voice, pacing, or unable to stay calm? That's who they will see as the threat. It doesn't matter if you are holding a paper.

First impressions matter, and right now, so does controlling yourself. Take three deep breaths to ground yourself, and don't lose your cool. The judge will know what happened, and that will determine the judge's decision on keeping the kids safe. Stay steady to protect your right to be in their lives.

I know you've been betrayed, and it feels like you shouldn't have to prove a damn thing. But courtrooms don't run on moral high ground. Judges rule based on evidence, behavior, and what serves the law and the children's best interest.

...and kids? They will remember how you show up, not just what happened to you.

Actions speak louder than words.

Stay flexible.

Show support.

...And prove -to the court and your kids, that you are the steady, positive presence they need.

You didn't end up as a custodial parent? Let's get one thing straight: your role as a parent is far from over.

In fact, now is your time to step up in new ways!

Be present. Show up. Work with the custodial parent to create the best situation for your kid. Ask how you can support, and make it clear you are willing to help in ways that work for everyone involved.

It's not about having the most time, it's about making the time count. Your kids need to know they can still rely on you, even if life looks a little different now.

Adaptability, and the ability to tune in emotionally and mentally, are your best allies. Pay attention to how your children are doing and what they need. Be available to talk, but patient with their timing.

Real, effective conversations happen when the moment feels right.

When is that? It's not tied to events, it's tied to emotional and mental openness of your kids. Wait for it.

Crisis Control Under the Same Roof

While this is an incredibly overwhelming time in your life, try not to behave in a way that might make others see you as the crazy one. If the police arrive during an altercation. Even if you have an order of protection, the officers won't initially know who the aggressor is. They simply see a conflict between two people.

Remember, their primary role is to ensure safety, including their own. The person who is visibly more agitated or making a scene usually gets pegged as the bigger threat, which is logical. So, stay calm and composed, show them you are not the one losing it.

I totally understand that in such situations, your anxiety level will be skyrocketing. The quickest, most effective trick? Take a couple of deep breaths through your nose. It's closer to the amygdala, which means it works faster at kicking in those anti-stress hormones.

Want more grounding techniques? Check out my YouTube channel for more resources. In the meantime, instead of being reactive to the situation around you, be proactive and work towards your goal.

I know this won't be easy. Start by calmly answering the police's questions. Stick to the facts, be patient, and make sure your side of the story is heard. Also, don't forget to get the name and badge number of the officer you are speaking with, and any witnesses you see around.

...Yes, I am repeating myself, because some truths are that important.

It's tough, but try to step back from the intensity of the moment. Take deep breaths to stay grounded. The calmer you stay, the better your chances of steering things in the right direction. You have got this.

However painful infidelity and breakups may be, finding a way to build a friendly -or at least cordial- relationship after divorce can seriously lighten the load. If kids are involved, it's a game-changer. It helps them heal and adapt so much easier. Divorce puts a lot on their tiny shoulders. Their whole world flips upside down, living between two homes, juggling schedules, and basically becoming nomads. It's tough on them, no doubt about it. If you can keep things civil, you are not just doing yourself a favor, you are doing them a huge one too.

So, here are a few rules on how to manage this time:

1. Curfews and Bedtimes: When to Power Down

Let's face it–kids think they don't need sleep, but we all know better. Set a bedtime routine that works for weekdays and weekends.

Weekdays? Lights out early enough so they don't look like zombies at school.

Weekends? Fine, give them a little wiggle room, but don't let it turn into an all-night Netflix binge. I assure you, their future selves will thank you for the consistency.

2. Freedoms and Privileges: Balancing Trust and Limits

Screen time? Parties? Electronics? It's a battlefield out there. Instead of micromanaging, lay down clear, simple rules that apply to everyone

....and stick to them!

The moment you break them, it's no longer a rule, it's a suggestion… and you'll find yourself negotiating every little battle.

No, the computer doesn't belong in their room. It belongs where you can see what's coming through that digital backdoor. Headphones? Cool–but you should still know what's piping into their ears. Better safe than sorry.

And tech? Not for hours on end. Full stop.

Also, let's talk safety: have a codeword they can use if they need an out at a party. Remind them you are their safety net, not their warden. Let them know they can count on you, without making freedom feel like a trap.

3. Chores and Responsibilities: Building Accountability

If they live there, they contribute. Period. Dishes, trash, walking the dog, pick your poison, but make sure they are helping. Studies prove that kids who do chores grow up more resourceful and better prepared for life outside your house. And if allowance is part of the deal? Tie it to effort, not entitlement. Life doesn't hand out freebies, and neither should you.

4. Discipline: Consistency Is Key

Kids are natural-born lawyers. They'll exploit every loophole if you let them. That's why your rules need to be rock-solid and consistent. Decide what counts as serious and what's minor. Big offenses? Big consequences. Little slip-ups? Teachable moments. But whatever you do, stand united–don't be the parent they pit against each other.

5. Education: Teaming Up for Their Future

Here's the truth: education isn't just about grades, it's about preparing a child to stand strong on their own two feet when the time comes. That's the goal. Not perfect report cards or gold stars, but raising someone who can handle life.

And let's face it, the new generation isn't exactly rushing to help mom and dad hold it all together. So how do we do this? It doesn't have to be complicated–just consistent. We show up. We create learning moments. But we don't do the work for them. We send the message: "I'm invested in your success," whatever that looks like for them.

Showing up isn't just about being there–it's about saying, *You matte*r. And that kind of message? It sticks. It shapes how your kids see themselves. And take my word for it, they are watching.

My mom never finished high school because of her asthma. I'll never forget her running the parents' 1000-meter race. She used to say, "It's not about coming in first–it's about not being last." And with asthma, she still pulled it off.

When she showed up at school, I felt proud–not because she brought treats or made a fuss, but because her presence told me I mattered.

That kind of validation doesn't fade. It becomes part of your kids' backbone.

6. Healthcare: Their Health, Your Unity

Check-ups, dentist appointments, emergency plans–it's all part of the gig. Divide the responsibilities and make sure you are clear on who's handling what. Oh, and don't forget their mental health. Your kids are dealing with a lot, and being proactive about their emotional well-being now saves everyone pain down the road.

7. Religious Practices: Navigating Faith and Values

If religion's part of your family's life, decide how it fits in post-breakup. Whether it's holiday traditions, attending services, or religious education, keep it consistent so your kids feel supported–not caught in the middle of competing values.

8. Communication: Keeping Everyone in the Loop

Who texts first when they are at the other parent's house? What's the emergency protocol? Get this straight now, so you are not fighting about it later. Clarity in communication makes everyone's life easier.

9. Holidays and Vacations: Sharing the Joys (and the Schedule)

Let's stop treating holidays like hostage negotiations. They're not prizes to win or chances to prove a point. They're meant to be joyful, for the kids and for everyone else around them.

Figure out what truly matters to you.

Figure out what you can live without.

And agree to meet somewhere in the messy, human middle.

Take turns. Be fair. Don't dig your heels in just to make a point. But also, don't always be the one who gives in just to keep the peace. That kind of imbalance builds quiet resentment, and the kids can feel it too.

...And for heaven's sake, avoid being the parent who turns a birthday cake into battlefield debris.

The goal isn't perfection.

It's peace.

It's giving your kids, and everyone else present, a chance to feel relaxed, safe, and maybe even a little joyful.

Because those are the moments they'll remember.

...And so will you.

10. Extracurriculars: Don't Overdo It

Sports are great, music lessons are wonderful, and theater can be life-changing. But let's not pretend more is always better. I've seen kids with a packed schedule every day of the week. They are drained, you are exhausted, and nobody is enjoying it.

Kids need downtime. Their bodies are growing, their brains are working overtime, and they're learning how to navigate the world. If you are running yourself ragged playing chauffeur, maybe it's time to ask: are they actually enjoying all this, or are you just keeping up appearances? Balance, my friends. A little structure and a lot of breathing room go a long way.

PARENTING TOGETHER? ...BARELY

It's been rough, and you are not just worried about yourself ...you are worried about your kids. No amount of protecting can fully hide what happened.

So here's my take: We all come into this world exposed to challenges we're meant to face, not avoid. That's how we build inner resources, character, and tools for life.

If we do the work early, we're better equipped to go after what we want, snap right back and keep going when things get tough.

The early years of life are exactly for that: learning to bounce back. That's why time off and real play –no screens, no competitive sports– matter so much.

Engaged with action figures or stuffed animals? That is storytelling that explores relationships, fears, fantasies, and even power struggles.

Pretending to be 'the parent'? That's not just mimicry. It's how kids work through power, care, and conflict. It's a way to emotionally digest their experiences, to make sense of the adult world using their own language of play.

Playing chase or hide-and-seek? That's such a rich game! A rehearsal for attachment. It's the thrill of being pursued, the fear of being forgotten, and the relief of being found again. It teaches that separation isn't abandonment, and that connection can survive distance.

This is why playing at home is so important. It's in those unstructured, safe environments that kids learn through trial and error, working through emotional stuff without even realizing it.

Those moments? They build the internal resources that will hold them up later on. Whether it's not getting what they want, facing disappointment, or losing a job. Learning to recover is what prepares us all for the hardest days.

And here is a fact: you can't be attached to their side 24/7 for the rest of their life. Nor should either of you want that, it's just not healthy.

Part of parenting is preparing them to face the world on their own terms, knowing they have the tools to stand back up when life knocks them down. It's about giving them the room and time to find footing on their own. You are present, steady, and supportive… not scrambled or overbearing.

That said, play alone is not going to cut it.

It's time to release the guilt and reset your mindset.

Prepare yourself not just to survive betrayal, but to succeed beyond it. And once you believe in that. Once it's etched into your DNA, you'll pass it on without even trying.

In the way you show up.

In the way you speak.

In the way your kids know, deep down, they've got what it takes.

Kids -especially teenagers- are walking a tightrope every single day, balancing emotions, school pressures, fears of bullying, body image struggles, and the weight of an uncertain future. Your role in this story? You are their safety net.

If that net's full of holes -empty promises, inconsistent rules, petty fights, one parent undermining the other, your kid might fall. When they do, it's a pain you know all too well.

Betrayal already blown your trust and left wounds that feel impossible to heal. Watching your children stumble as a result? That cuts deeper yet. That's why before you act, ask yourself these basic questions that are good for all parenting and even good for you:

Am I parenting with intention, or just reacting? It's common in the rush and noise to give situational answers without seeing the big picture. The smallest actions today leave a lasting mark.

Is this the healthiest choice for my child's growth, or just the easiest right now?

Does this build my child's strength, confidence, or real-life skills, or just keep things comfortable?

Am I making this choice out of guilt, or because it truly sets my child up for success?

Is this actually good for my child, or does it just look good to others? Choose life over display.

Nothing works without respect. Respect is the foundation, the value that organizes behavior and interaction, creating a natural hierarchy of what's acceptable and what is not. If kids don't learn to respect you, they won't truly respect anyone... not even themselves, as I told you before.

These questions apply to any parent, not just those co-parenting. But now, let's get into the ground rules for this messy, imperfect phase of 'parenting together, barely.'

If you are here, you are already trying, and that's where it all begins. Take a moment to go through the following steps designed specifically for navigating life after infidelity and betrayal.

This toolkit? It's a quick-start guide, but if you are ready to go deeper, I've got you. You'll find the full Co-Parenting Playbook with expanded strategies, scripts, and age-specific advice on my website.

In the meantime, here are the five non-negotiables for raising healthy kids after betrayal:

Your Kids Are Not Weapons: Don't use them to score points or settle scores.

They're Not Messengers Either: If you've got something to say, pick up the phone. Drop the "Tell your mom/dad..." routine.

No Badmouthing the Other Parent: No judging, nor criticizing... Ever. Even if your new ex isn't your kids' parent. Even if you believe every word is the gospel truth.... even if it burns to hold it back.

If it stings, zip it up!

Say less.

Heal more.

Because no matter how deep the pain runs, you can't let it pull you into bitterness. You've got too much to rebuild. Starting with yourself.

Keep it neutral and let your kids have the relationship they deserve with both their parents.

Adult Problems Stay With Adults: Kids don't need to be in the middle. Let them be kids, it's not their job to carry your baggage.

Don't make them pick between parents: Don't make them pick between parents. It's cruel. It's unnecessary. It can actually leave scars. Growing up with a negative image of a parent? That's not healthy for anyone. Besides, your relationship with your partner is not your kids'. Kids thrive when they can love both parents freely. Protect their emotional foundation by keeping your conflicts out of their world

If your old teens want to stay with the unfaithful parent, let them (as long as it's safe, even if you believe your ex is a narcissist).

There's no point in fighting it.

If you force them to stay with you, in the long run, you'll be the one losing. They'll remember, and they will hold it against you.

Instead, make sure they know you love them, and that your door is always wide open if they ever want to come back. But it is also not a revolving door that lets in manipulation games.

Children -as we all do- learn from experience. Keep your cool and let them see their betraying parent's inconsistencies for themselves. They'll figure it out.

Don't push them to pick sides. Be patient. Parents who've played the long game often face some lonely stretches, but soon enough, their kids come back.

Older.

Wiser.

...And seeing things way clearer!

Got any doubts along the way? Remember to picture your kid in therapy at 30, spilling about their life while growing up. What do you want them to say to their therapist?

Didn't get enough? Well, that's what the website's for.

Dive into another F. Freud book,
follow Dr Roth's FΨck Freud podcast:
Shrink Me? I'm Just Waking Up.
Visit her www.drliaroth.com/LR2 website
or go to her YouTube channel
for more insights and tools to reclaim your bold.

About the Author

Dr. Lia A. Roth, a psychoanalyst with a wealth research, academic and clinical background, combines her deep expertise in the complex world of the human mind and relationships.

With a psychology degree from the University of Buenos Aires and advanced studies at Washington University in St. Louis and the Boston Graduate School of Psychoanalysis, she knows her way around the messy minds and twisted emotions we all try to hide.

Her new book? It's a fire-starting manifesto for anyone who's been spinning in the middle of a relationship without moving forward. Stuck in the 'gray zone'? Dr. Roth says that's no place to be. Here's the deal: it's not about giving an inch, taking a mile, or lying down for the sake of so-called "compromise." No way. If you are selling out your own dreams just to keep the peace, you are not living in love, you are surviving. Which is a huge difference.

Dr. Roth dives into her 'binary relationship theory,' blowing up the idea that love is a compromise. It's a dynamic balance where it's all about you, me, *and* the spark we're creating together. If it's dead, if it's toxic, if it's stealing your vibe: fix it or nix it, but for the love of sanity, don't just hang around hoping it'll magically get better. That's what this book is here to shake out of you.

And betrayal? Oh, it's deeper than "someone did me wrong." Dr. Roth cracks it open, betrayal doesn't just crush trust; it shakes you to your core, twisting your sense of self until you barely recognize who you are ..and, no, this isn't some PTSD story. It's an identity crisis, a total wake-up to everything you are made of. Drawing from semiotic theory (yup, the study of signs and symbols), she shows you how betrayal strikes on a level most people don't even see coming.

Loaded with Dr. Roth's no-BS insights, raw stories, and a big punch of sass, this book gives you the map to escape the cycle, regain your confidence, and walk out stronger than ever. This isn't just some feel-good read; it's your blueprint to take control, live bigger, and find the strength you never knew you had. If this feels uncomfortable, good. Growth is supposed to stretch you!

BIBLIOGRAPHY

AbiNader MA, Graham LM, Kafka JM. (2023). Examining Intimate Partner Violence-Related Fatalities: Past Lessons and Future Directions Using U.S. National Data. Journal of Family Violence, 12:1-12. doi: 10.1007/s10896-022-00487-2. Epub ahead of print. PMID: 36685752; PMCID: PMC9838333.

Bion, W. R. (1987). *Second thoughts: Selected papers on psychoanalysis. London:* Routledge.

Brown, B. (2015). *Daring greatly: How the courage to be vulnerable transforms the way we live, love, parent, and lead*. Avery.

Chandler, D. (2007). *Semiotics: The basics* (2nd ed.). Routledge.

Damasio, A. R. (1999). The feeling of what happens: Body and emotion in the making of consciousness. London, UK: Vintage.

Damasio, A. R. (2010). Self comes to mind: Constructing the conscious brain. New York, NY: Pantheon Books.

Doidge, N. (2007). *The brain that changes itself: Stories of personal triumph from the frontiers of brain science.* Viking Penguin.

Doidge, N. (2015). *The brain's way of healing: Remarkable discoveries and recoveries from the frontiers of neuroplasticity.* Viking Penguin.

Freyd, J., & Birrell, P. (2013). *Blind to betrayal: Why we fool ourselves we aren't being fooled*. Trade Paper Press.

Gieles, N. C., Gerritse, K., Zandbergen, E., Both, S., & Kreukels, B. P. C. (2024). "No one told me how this could be pleasurable" A Qualitative Focus Group Study into Experiences and Needs of Transgender People in Addressing Sexuality in the Context of Gender-Affirming Medical Care in The Netherlands. *Journal of Sex & Marital Therapy*, 1-21. https://doi.org/10.1080/0092623X.2024.2402315.

González Taboas, C. (2024). Seminario *Amar no es hacerse amar: goce, amor, deseo*. Buenos Aires, Argentina.

Hartmann, H. (1958). *Ego psychology and the problem of adaptation* (D. Rapaport, Trans.). International Universities Press. (Original work published 1939).

Herman, J. L. (2022). *Trauma and recovery: The aftermath of violence–from domestic abuse to political terror.* Basic Books.

Hollenbeck, Ed.D., LMHC, C. M., & Steffens, Ph.D, B. (2024). Betrayal Trauma Anger: Clinical Implications for Therapeutic Treatment based on the Sexually Betrayed Partner's Experience Related to Anger after Intimate Betrayal. *Journal of Sex & Marital Therapy,* 50(4), 456-467. https://doi.org/10.1080/0092623X.2024.2306940.

Horton Cooley, C. (1902). Human Nature and the Social Order. New York: Scribner's, pp. 179-185.

Jonason, P. K., & Webster, G. D. (2010). The dirty dozen: A concise measure of the dark triad. *Psychological Assessment,* 22(2), 420-432

Karimi R, Bakhtiyari M, Masjedi Arani A. Protective factors of marital stability in long-term marriage globally: a systematic review. Epidemiol Health. 2019;41:e2019023. doi: 10.4178/epih.e2019023. Epub 2019 Jun 15. PMID: 31208194; PMCID: PMC6702121.

Kohut, H. (1972). Thoughts on Narcissism and Narcissistic Rage. Psychoanalytic Study of the Child. 27:360-400.

Langer, S. K. (1967). *Mind: An essay on human feeling* (Vol. 1). Johns Hopkins University Press.

Nietzsche, F. (2008). *Twilight of the idols: Or, how to philosophize with a hammer* (P. Smith, Trans.). Barnes & Noble. (Original work published 1888).

Peirce, C. S. (1986). *La ciencia de la semiótica* (A. Zalamea, Ed.). Nueva Visión.

Porges, S. W. (2009). The polyvagal theory: New insights into adaptive reactions of the autonomic nervous system. *Cleveland Clinic Journal of Medicine*, 76(4), S86S90.

Rokach, A., & Chan, S. H. (2023). Love and infidelity: Causes and consequences. *International Journal of Environmental Research and Public Health, 20*(5), 3904. https://doi.org/10.3390/ijerph20053904.

Roth, L. (2020). *Psychoanalytic Perspectives on Gaze, Body Image, Shame, Judgment and Maternal Function: Being and Belonging*. Routledge, U.K.

Solms, M. (2013). The conscious id. *Neuro-Psychoanalysis, 15*(1), 5-19.

Wiest, B. (2020). The mountain is you: Transforming self-sabotage into self-mastery. Thought Catalog Books.

What People Are Saying...

Amazon Customer: I am a lawyer. I'm no stranger to making tough calls. But relationships? That's a whole different battlefield. Get In or Get Out but Don't Stay in the Freakin' Middle hit me like a wake-up call I didn't know I needed (...)

La Lishy: A Lifeline for the Brokenhearted: I've endured the devastation of infidelity and betrayal. Get In or Get Out but Don't Stay in the Freakin' Middle felt like the friend I never had during my darkest moments. Dr. Lia Roth gives you the clarity and tools to face the storm head-on and come out stronger.

Harry T: This book feels like that no-nonsense friend who tells you what you need to hear, even if it stings. I wish I had it 30 years ago. Dr. Lia Roth doesn't sugarcoat betrayal or the messy in-between. She hands you a flashlight, points to the exit, and says, 'Your move.' It's not about fixing someone else, it's about reclaiming yourself. Sharp, funny, and empowering. If you are stuck, this is the push you need.

Brodi Miller: Dr. Roth, opens up the book with a powerful story of how she had to overcome extreme betrayal, which helps you relate to her in a human way. On top of that her deep knowledge and expertise in this feed. I personally love the line "Failure is not the choice you've made. The real failure is living a life that never felt like yours to begin with." Lots of other great line and lots of wisdom in this book. Highly recommended.

Sir Marco Robinson: Dr lia Roth has really nailed what betrayal can do to you if you stay indecisive... a book about making the best out of yourself ... and then really understanding if you should be with this person you are with. Given that relationships make or break us. This is a very important book.

Finished this book? Don't stop here!

Your turn: Pen down. Power up!

Made in United States
Orlando, FL
08 May 2025

61143641R00164